Carl A. Levenson

Socrates
Among the Corybantes

Being, Reality, and the Gods

SPRING PUBLICATIONS
THOMPSON, CONN.

In memory of
BENJAMIN CRAIN LEVENSON (1918–1998),
my father and a musician,
and in honor of SYLVIA PISNER LEVENSON,
my mother

Published by Spring Publications
Thompson, Conn.
www.springpublications.com

Copyright © 1999, 2022 by Spring Publications and Carl A. Levenson
All rights reserved

First published in 1999
Second, revised edition 2022

Cover image:
Inscribed Herm of Socrates
Naples, National Archaeological Museum

Library of Congress Control Number: 2022901886
ISBN: 978-0-88214-960-8

CONTENT

PREFACE 9

CHAPTER ONE
A Brief Sketch of the Euthydemus 13

CHAPTER TWO
The Euthydemus in Previous Commentaries 29

CHAPTER THREE
The First Socratic Discourse 39

CHAPTER FOUR
The Second Socratic Discourse 49

CHAPTER FIVE
Two, not One, or The Chairing of Cleinias 61

CHAPTER SIX
The Harrowing Transition 77

CHAPTER SEVEN
The Final Revelation 99

CHAPTER EIGHT
Conclusion 153

AFTERWORD (2022)
Politics and Philosophy 165

ACKNOWLEDGMENTS 174

As it befell Parmeniscus in the legend, who in the cave of Trophonius lost the power to laugh, but got it again on the island of Delos, at the sight of the shapeless block exhibited their as the image of the goddess Leto, so it has befallen me. When I was young, I forgot how to laugh in the cave of Trophonius; when I was older, I opened my eyes and beheld reality, at which I began to laugh, and since then I have not stopped laughing.

SØREN KIERKEGAARD, Either/Or

We must recognize the presence in Plato...of a peculiar vein of freakish humor.

A. E. TAYLOR, Plato

PREFACE

In Plato's dialogues, we find many references to the Corybantic rites, rites of initiation performed in honor of the goddess Rhea. But the *Euthydemus*, I suggest, does more than refer to the rites. Within the context of Socratic dialectic, it presents the rite itself, an actual performance of the rite—veiled and distorted, to be sure, but there nevertheless.

This view of the *Euthydemus*—that it secretly presents a Corybantic initiation—is not, as far as I know, suggested by any other commentator. The *Euthydemus* is usually presented as a satire on philosophic wrangling. It is, of course, also that. And almost always it is relegated to a marginal place in Plato's canon.

The dialogue, if I am right about it, is a valuable source for the history of religion. The rites of the Corybantes were assuredly meant to be secret. Plato, in some sense, "lets the cat out of the bag." And since the Corybantic rites are of the Dionysian kind, Plato gives us a glimpse of the reality of Dionysian ecstasy. We can learn from Plato how the ecstasy felt; no other ancient writer dares to tell us.

From the point of view of philosophy, the *Euthydemus* helps us to "rethink" the dialogues of Plato. For all those who insist that Plato is too rational, that he has abstracted us from the world, has rejected it in favor of the forms—Plato here proposes a different mode of deliverance; the way of intimacy with the world, of matter rather than form. For complete immersion in the material substrate of the world (through music, dance, erotic feelings, etc.) is what Plato discovered in the Dionysian ecstasy, but the aim of the ecstasy (as Plato comments in the *Phaedrus* [244c]), is to "purify" the soul of "ancient evil."

All things considered, the *Euthydemus* has much to teach us, but the teaching is disguised by Plato's presentation. It is disguised because it includes the secrets of a cult. It is disguised because it could easily be misinterpreted. It is disguised because Plato is fond of disguises, for there is an artistic element in Plato of which everyone is more or less aware.

Our task, of course, is to take away the disguise, and I believe we can manage this successfully. Hints about the meaning of the dialogue may be found on almost every page. The explicit content of the dialogue—the mad use of fallacy, the grotesque and hideous imagery, the obscene jokes, the odd behavior of Socrates—all these things, which can easily be interpreted from the point of view I am proposing, make no sense at all if the dialogue is merely what it seems.

The *Euthydemus*, as I have said, has always occupied a marginal place in Plato's canon, but I have learned so much from my study of it, that I think it should be considered one of Plato's most important works. Many curious things in Plato take on meaning in its light: the frequent allusions to the Corybantes, the famous praise of *mania*, the shifting perspective on Socrates, the harsh critique of tragedy, the notorious interest in the number two or "dyad," the odd deliverances about being and non-being. All these things and many more, which often puzzle the thoughtful reader of Plato, will be clarified, I hope, in the present study.

Above all there is this: the *Euthydemus* provides a corrective to the "escapist" view of Plato—to Heidegger's view, for example, that Plato "turns away from being." Having studied the *Euthydemus*, I can say with absolute certainty that Plato is unflinching, that he turns away from nothing, that he has faced, more than anyone, sheer being in its excess and pain.

The magician Virgil had himself cut into pieces and put into a kettle to be boiled for a week, in order to renew his youth. He hired a man to stand watch so that no intruder would peep into the cauldron. But the watchman could not resist the temptation: it was too early: Virgil banished with a cry like a little child.

SØREN KIERKEGAARD, Either/Or

CHAPTER ONE

A Brief Description of the Euthydemus

1. *Socrates Vanished*

> By some providence I happened to be sitting there—there where you saw me, in the undressing room, quite alone—and I had it in mind to get up and go. But just as I was getting up, there came the daimon's usual sign. So I sat down again, and a bit later, two persons came in, Euthydemus and Dionysodorus, and also quite a number of their pupils—or so it seemed to me. The two men came in and started walking around in the cloister (Plato, *Euthydemus*, 273a).[1]

Socrates's daimon is a spiritual presence, assigned to him at birth. It "signals" or "speaks" to him, and he feels this in his mind. It never urges him forward but always holds him back when he is about to make the wrong move (*Apology*, 31d), and it thereby insures that his life take the shape for which it was destined.[2] Plato associates the daimon with an image of Socrates him-

---

1. The translation is mine. My aim is readability with a decent rhythm. On the opposite side of my translation is the Loeb edition, translated by W. R. M. Lamb. It is not a close translation and has "aged" over the years but retains its grace. I "raided it frequently." For an accurate translation of the dialogue, see Plato, *Euthydemus*, trans. R. K. Sprague (New York, Bobbs-Merrill, 1965); Sprague's notes are excellent.
2. In the *Republic*, Book X, 620e, the role of the daimon is presented mythically, as follows: "When all the souls had chosen their lives, they went before Lachesis. And she sent with each, as the guardian of his life and the fullfiller of his choice, the daimon that he had chosen, and the divinity led the soul

self, a kind of superior second Socrates installed within Socrates's own consciousness.³ What Socrates is to the city, so the daimon is to him—an exhorter, a critic, and a summoner.

Thanks to the daimon, Socrates does not depart too soon on the day described in the *Euthydemus*. There is nothing going on in the undressing room. He finds himself sitting alone and has just decided to leave. But as soon as he gets up, he feels the presence of the daimon resisting him. He yields to this, as always. For the daimon apprehends the whole of his life—all the years, past and future, together—and its promptings (read correctly) cannot fail to be beneficial.

To describe the events that follow is not an easy task for the *Euthydemus*, among Plato's dialogues, is rivaled only by the *Laws* in its strangeness. But I will offer a few notes and try to convey a brief impression—a provisional impression to be sure, but fair as far as it goes.

The dominant figures in the dialogue, who appear suddenly after the daimon signals to Socrates, are the Thurian brothers, Euthydemus and Dionysodorus. They are supposed to be sophists, but they are more like clowns—the clowns of a bad dream—huge, vulgar, and threatening. They tell bad jokes about murder, muti-

---

first to Clotho, under her hand and her turning of the spindle to ratify the destiny of his lot and choice, and after contact with her, the daimon again led the soul to the spinning of Atropos to make the web of its destiny irreversible, and then without a backward look it passed beneath the throne of Necessity." Quoted by James Hillman in *The Soul's Code: In Search of Character and Calling* (New York: Random House, 1996). Hillman interprets: "The soul of each of us is given a unique daimon before we are born, and it has selected an image or pattern that we live on earth...The daimon remembers what is in your image and belongs to your pattern, and therefore the daimon is the carrier of your destiny" (8). In all of Plato's writing, only one Socratic conversation is warranted by the daimon, that in the *Euthydemus*.

3. See *Hippias Major*, 286b, 288d, 292d, 304c. The "friend" described there who haunts Socrates's mental life, criticizes his wisdom, goads and exhorts him, lives in the same house, comes from the same family, and is so impertinent that one frequently wishes to "kill" him, is obviously a double of Socrates himself, and his function is that of the daimon.

lation, voyeurism, deicide—we need not pile up examples of the weirdness. Their jokes, however repellent, always bring laughter from the audience, for they travel with a "chorus," a crowd of adoring pupils, whom they have carefully trained to laugh on cue (276c). It is the first "canned" laughter in literature.

The encounter, as it progresses, grows wilder, more embarrassing. It is soon out of control and mounting toward a climax that threatens to be horrific. We expect Socrates to do something, to put on the brakes, to restore order, and clarity. We expect him here, as in other dialogues, to defeat his opponents in the end.

However, this never happens. Socrates, in fact, does not know how to deal with the brothers. He thinks that perhaps he ought to "refute" their jokes, so he anticipates the punch lines (which makes him seem like a bad sport) and points out logical errors (whereas jokes don't have to be logical). The brothers simply ignore him. Or else, they reproach him with disobeying the rules—for they seem to be acquainted with elaborate rules of debate that suppress any opposition to them (295–96). One feels, finally, that the only way to defeat the brothers would be to go away, to scorn their astonishing performance. But Socrates stays and struggles, deterred by the daimon from leaving.

He does, it is true, interrupt the brothers on two separate occasions, and he gives the crowd a sample of his own manner of thought. But unfortunately he is a skeptical thinker, so he has no positive truth to oppose to the brothers' games. And when at last he shows what he most wants to show, which is that he knows nothing, but "knows that he doesn't know," the brothers laugh out loud and swear to reveal what he does not know. We have the terrible feeling that they can.

At the end of the performance, the audience cheers the brothers, and Socrates, too, cheers them. What the daimon foresaw has most emphatically come to pass. In no other text does Plato describe such tremendous applause; the very pillars quake with admiration (308b).

2. What the Brothers Say

The central point of the *Euthydemus* lies hidden behind its strangeness; therefore, any discussion of the dialogue should let the strangeness appear in all its force. In this respect, it is best to let the text speak for itself.

Here, then, by way of introduction, I offer a selection from the *Euthydemus*, along with some preliminary comments; all will be taken up again in later chapters. The key is to remember that nonsense need not be frivolous, merely because it is nonsense. The most horrendous notions certainly may (and possibly must) be expressed in nonsensical ways.

Let us note, first of all, that the brothers claim to teach virtue—and they make this claim in a particularly startling way.

> Virtue, Socrates, is what we claim to teach—and our method is beautiful and swift.
>
> By Zeus! That's not a small matter! (273d)

To make people virtuous is a task that eludes even the best teacher; to make people virtuous in a swift and beautiful way is perhaps a task that eludes even a god. By what art can the brothers make people virtuous? Socrates wants to know (his own claims for teaching are modest), and the brothers are happy to demonstrate their method—a method consisting of jokes and extravagant claims.

Here, for example, is a joke about murdering Cleinias, an attractive youth whom everyone likes and respects. A certain philosophic meaning may perhaps be found in the joke, but this seems poor compensation for its tastelessness.

> Tell me, Socrates, said Dionysodorus, do you want this youth to become wise?
>
> Certainly, I said.
>
> Well is he wise now or not?
>
> He says he's not…
>
> So what he's not, you want him to be. And what he is, you want him to stop being. You want him dead! Why what

excellent friends and lovers you are! You desire your darling dead at any price! (283*c–d*)

Here are some claims, so extravagant they make one giddy, concerning truth, knowledge, and power. All these claims are supported by "arguments," which we will discuss in subsequent chapters.

> Look here, Dionysodorus, I said, the substance of your statement is that there is no such thing as speaking falsely...
>
> He agreed...
>
> Then there is no false opinion, I said... Nor ignorance, nor ignorant men...
>
> None, he said. (286*c–d*)
>
> Then, do you two really know everything? I asked.
>
> Certainly, he said...
>
> The stars, Dionysodorus... do you know how many there are? And have you numbered the grains of sand?
>
> Certainly, he said. (294*b*)
>
> But I don't suppose, I said, that you have gone so far in wisdom as to be able to do a sword dance...
>
> There is nothing, he replied, that I cannot do. (294*e*)

None of this, however, entirely conveys the strangeness of the performance, which rapidly degenerates into a kind of slapstick comedy with absurd, sinister themes. Here, for example, the brothers take hold of their opponents' words, rearranging them in such a way as to bring about the images they wish to provoke—images of brutality toward those one loves. The interlocutor here is Ctesippus, a shrewd and aggressive youth.

> Just tell me, Ctesippus, said Dionysodorus, have you a dog?
>
> Yes, a real rogue.
>
> And has he pups?
>
> Yes, a set of rogues like him.
>
> Then is the dog their father?
>
> Yes. I saw him with my own eyes, covering the bitch.

> Then he is a father and yours, and so—a dog is your father. You are the brother of whelps! And one point more: do you beat this dog?
>
> God yes! Since I can't beat you...
>
> Why, then, you beat your father! (298d–e)

Another joke, which equivocates at some length on the concept of "the good," generates a ghastly, but rich and complicated, image. Skulls, gilded and filled with gold, were prized by the Skythians;[4] but the experience of seeing one's own gilded skull comes from the world of archaic rites and ordeals, where it appears as an expression of spiritual perfection.[5]

> You agree, do you not, said Dionysodorus, that gold is a good thing?
>
> I do, replied Ctesippus.
>
> Why, then, we ought always to have it, and everywhere, and above all in ourselves. So we shall be happiest if three talents of gold are stuffed in our belly, and a talent in our skull, and a stater in each of our eyes.
>
> You are right, sir! You are right! For the happiest men in Skythia, they say, have vast amounts of gold in their "own" skulls...and a still more marvelous thing is told, how they drink from their skulls when gilded, and how they gaze inside them, holding them in their hands (299d–e).

Exchanges of this sort are typical of the dialogue—the dialogue is full of them; it exists, so to say, to present them. The last joke in the dialogue, which is perhaps the most repellent, is explicitly "religious" in theme.

> You have gods, Socrates? asked Dionysodorus...Apollo, Zeus, and Athena...
>
> Certainly, I said...

---

4. See Herodotus, *Histories*, IV.65.

5. See Mircea Eliade, *Shamanism: Archaic Techniques of Ecstasy* (Princeton, N.J.: Princeton University Press, 1972), passim.

> And the gods, I presume, are animals. For you have admitted that whatever is animate is animal. Or are the gods deprived of life?
>
> They have life…
>
> Come, then, and tell me: since, as you agree, Zeus and the other gods are yours…you can sell them, bestow them, and treat them just as you please…just like your other animals…
>
> Bravo, Hercules! Ctesippus cried.
>
> And here, everyone who was present…wildly extolled the argument and the two men; and all nearly died of laughing, clapping, and rejoicing. (302*d*–303*b*)

Now, let us gather all this up into a question. Suppose two men come up to you and say that they have a method, a swift, beautiful method, of "improving" you and making you "virtuous." You reply (having received a divine sign) that you are interested in the experience. The men then tell you that you can do anything you like, absolutely anything, and that you know everything, too, and always have and always will. They then go on to insinuate that these new powers of yours are peculiarly related to your desire to kill those you love, to your close affinity to beasts, to your longing to be murdered, gilded, and decapitated, and to your plan to execute God, whom you have come to view as "your animal." What would you make of these men?

In all commentaries known to me, the brothers are presented as caricatures of popular educators, or bad logicians, or masters of the art of disputation. Socrates, we are told, earnestly strives to reach truth, but the brothers only want to amaze and confuse their hearers. That is why they argue in an irresponsible way.

However, this view leaves many questions unanswered. As caricatures of sophists, the brothers argue irresponsibly, but this only explains the form of the discourse. It does not explain the content. It does not explain what they say. Why this particular content? Why not something quite different, something less distracting, perhaps? Is all the talk of knowledge and power, suffering and sacrifice, gilding, killing, decapitating, and so on—is all this arbitrary?

If not, what purpose does it serve within the dialogue? And finally, we ask, how are these subjects related to Plato's other dialogues and to his enterprise, in general?

3. The Brothers and the Corybantic Rites

The secret of the brothers is revealed in a comment of Socrates, to be found in our text at 277d. The background of the comment is as follows. Socrates has insisted that the youth Cleinias—an exemplary youth in whom everyone takes an interest—become a participant in the brothers' demonstration. "Have no fear," says Socrates, "perhaps your gain will be great" (275e). So Cleinias submits, and the brothers hit him with arguments. The arguments come at such a rapid rate that Cleinias does not know what to say.

Now comes Socrates's comment:

> Do not be surprised, my dear Cleinias, if the arguments of our visitors seem queer to you, for perhaps you do not see what they are doing to you. They are acting like the celebrants of the Corybantic rites, when they perform the chairing (*thronosis*) of the person they are going to initiate. There, as you know, if you have been through it, they have dancing and playing; and so these two are dancing and playing around you, as they prepare for your initiation. (277d)

The brothers, then, resemble ministers of the Corybantes. But who were the Corybantes?

We learn from this and other sources that the Corybantes were mystical warriors, devoted to Rhea (or Cybele). They danced a frenzied dance, with swords and in full armor, to the flute and the tambourine. It was said that, if you listened to their music and danced with them, you would experience power, knowledge, and joy.

One can discern the application to the brothers. The brothers are swordsmen (273e), and they are compared to dancers (276d). They say they can dance with swords (294e). Their discourse, moreover, is infectious, like music (301b, 303e), and they rave (as we noticed) about knowledge, power, and joy (293–94, 296d). Further, if we view the brothers as ministers of the Corybantes, we can begin to find a meaning in the strangeness of their performance. The hysterical laughter induced by them is a rough approximation of the mania caused by the rites. And the sadistic content of their jokes likewise becomes intelligible, for the Corybantic dancers, like the Bacchae whom they resembled, were known to have violent ways, since the power they worshiped was, as Euripides says, "Most terrible, though kindest, to men."[6]

Let us now reconsider the performance of the brothers, this time taking the view that it is modeled on the Corybantic rites. The performance divides in three parts, with Socrates speaking in the intervals. We will consider each in turn.

The first part of the performance is the "chairing" of Cleinias, the boy who plays the role of neophyte. The brothers (the initiators) "dance" around Cleinias, and shout strange things at him, and make him blush and feel disoriented. Soon, he looks like a wrestler "going down for the third fall" (277c).

The second part of the performance we will call "the harrowing transition." It is here that the new initiates pay the price of the knowledge they receive. Thus, the brothers invent a scenario in which Cleinias is to be murdered by the people who care most for him—by Ctesippus, his lover, and Socrates, his friend. "What excellent friends and lovers you are," the brothers cackle maniacally. "You desire your darling dead at any price" (283d)! Although Ctesippus and Socrates struggle against this scenario, in the dreamlike world that the brothers have established, the scenario seems to prevail, and Ctesippus and Socrates give in (285a).

In the third part of the performance—we will call it "the final revelation"—the brothers try to induce the intense ecstatic experience at which the rite aims. Socrates comments that this is the "serious" part of the rite (300e). Of what, then, does it consist?

---

6. *The Bacchae*, 860. The lines refer to Dionysus. Concerning Rhea, the Orphic poet speaks of her as the source of all bounty but also says that she rejoices in "frenzied fighting" and delights in "mankind's horrid screams." *Hymns of Orpheus*, XIII, XXVI.

In one way: clearly, it is a matter of regression. The brothers provoke a condition resembling "infantile megalomania." There is giddiness, dizziness, a sense of power and perfection, and a release from inhibitions and from shame (294*a*).

In another way—and from the point of view of ontology—we may say that it is a matter of letting being rise beyond its limits. Knowledge (293*b–d*), power (294*a–b*), time (296*a*), shame (294*d*), one's mother (298*d*), one's father (298*c*), a drug (298*b*), a bit of gold (299*e*)—all these things, and many more, overcome the limits that we normally impose on them and swell and converge at infinity.

In still another way—and this is perhaps what is most important—it is a matter of contemplating certain images—grotesque images charged with numinous power. There are men who turn into beasts, men who turn into giants, men with a hundred arms, men who gaze at their own skulls and fill them with wine and drink from them, and there is also the alchemist's dream—the dream of a world turned to gold—which is linked to these severed skulls (298–301). Further, there is the clamor of the forge and the crucible, there are three figures of culture (the smith, the potter, and the cook) who perish in a fire (a fire which they themselves kindle). Finally there are the gods (Zeus, Apollo, and Athena) who are transmuted into beasts (were they originally worshiped as beasts?) and placed on the sacrificial table (300*b*, 302). It is this last image—the gods sacrificed as beasts—that provokes the cry, "Bravo, Hercules!" and arouses such joy in the crowd.

4. *The Brothers Initiate Socrates*

Let us now step back for a moment and ask another question. How does Socrates respond to the Corybantic rite? It seems that, in an eerie, ambiguous way, he becomes increasingly entangled in it.

At first, he seems remote and unaffected; he merely watches the brothers quietly. Later, he starts to resist them. But his resistance is so ineffectual that it comes to seem giddy and fantastic—a part of the rite itself. At 301*b*, Socrates starts to talk like the brothers. At 302*b*, he feels their net close around him. At 303*b*, he "almost dies" applauding them along with the rest of the crowd.

Clearly, this is not the Socrates of the other dialogues, always in control, always directing the "performance" of the others. But what is the point of this involvement (submission?) of Socrates? The point is this—the brothers initiate Socrates. It is a fantastic initiation (the sort familiar in dreams), but it is effective.

First, we need to ask this. If the brothers initiate Socrates, they must have something to teach him. What is it, then, that they know?

As a matter of fact, the brothers appear to know the doctrines of Plato's middle-period—preexistence, recollection, immortality, etc.—whereas, in this dialogue, Socrates does not seem acquainted with them. Many commentators speak of this, and Friedlander and Hawtrey, among others, offer helpful discussions.[7] So we may say (speaking half-seriously) that the brothers teach Socrates Platonism. But why have they been assigned this task?

Consider the character of Socrates. He had, it seems, "detached" himself from being. He "rose" above being and looked down upon it critically. He wanted to decide what it was for. Aristophanes, in *The Clouds*, pictures him floating in a basket. He is staring into the sky, leaving earth, or being, behind.[8] Plato, in the *Euthydemus*, depicts him in much the same way. He is wandering "in a maze" (291b) and teasing himself like a child (292e), because he cannot find an art that will rise above all other arts and—"confer a use on all beings" (291d).

Of course, all this wandering and teasing is for the benefit of Cleinias, who will learn, at Socrates's hands, the limits of merely human wisdom. And yet Socrates feels, in his peculiar, ironic way, that the question of the usefulness of being calls for another type of teacher—and he therefore "bellows" for the brothers as if they were saviors and sons of Zeus (293a). But how can the brothers "save" Socrates and Cleinias?

---

7. See Chapter VII, note 10.

8. "I walk on air and contemplate the sun...By violence earth draws down the essence (*ikmada*) of our thinking (*The Clouds*, 225–35)." Note that, in Plato's middle period dialogues, the word "being" (*einai*) is made to refer, not to the concrete presence, the "earthiness," that Socrates shuns, but to the "forms" (*eide*) that he contemplates and thirsts for (*Republic*, 475e–477c). The *Euthydemus* helps bring about this shift.

The answer is that the brothers, as mystical fencers and dancers, disclose to all who listen an ecstatic vision of being. They do not, of course, "know" how to make being useful. But the art they practice, which causes being to rise in its fullness, solves the question of "use" all the same. Why does Plato imply that the brothers teach Socrates Platonism?

The answer is that, in spite of Heidegger and Nietzsche, one does not become a Platonist merely by "stepping outside" of being. One becomes a Platonist when, having "stepped outside" of being, one "bellows for the brothers" and plunges back into being again.

5. *Socrates Made Young and Beautiful*

Where, then, have we arrived? It seems that, in the dream-world of Platonism, the brothers are priests of the Corybantes, and they make Socrates one of their own. In support of this view, I will first bring forward an image from the *Euthydemus* and then speak of the place of the *Euthydemus* among Plato's other writings.

First, the image: the famous Medea of Colchis claimed to rejuvenate men by boiling them. It occurs to Socrates, in the middle of the *Euthydemus*, that he, too, could use a treatment of this sort. "I am an old man," he says, "and I am not afraid to take risks, and I put myself into the hands of Dionysodorus as if he were Medea of Colchis. Let him decimate me, let him do with me what he wants to, let him boil me down if he must (285c)."

So the brother's discourse is a thick, boiling brew in which Socrates is immersed, to be made young and beautiful again. Being boiled alive, as the history of religion tells us, often appears as a rite that confers renewal.[9] And to have created a new Socrates, a young and beautiful Socrates—this was the proud claim of Plato himself. Plato writes:

> It is impossible that what has been written should not be disclosed. That is why there is not and will not be any

---

9. See Mircea Eliade, *A History of Religious Ideas*, vol. 1: *From the Stone Age to the Eleusinian Mysteries*, trans. Willard R. Trask (Chicago: The University of Chicago Press, 1978), 371.

work of Plato's own. What are now called his works are the works of a Socrates made young and beautiful. Farewell and believe (*Epistle II*).

But, some will say, Medea of Colchis lied. She only claimed to restore men by boiling them. Actually, she only cooked them. Her victims were never seen again. Yes, that is true. Medea of Colchis lied. The image chosen by Plato expresses a certain pessimism. Plato's treatment, however, certainly succeeded with Socrates, and that brings us to our next point.

The *Euthydemus* is most probably a "late-early" dialogue. It was written at the threshold of Plato's middle period when he wrote his most beautiful works.[10] Now what is pertinent here is this. In the early dialogues, written before the *Euthydemus*, Socrates is brilliant and charismatic, but he is also irritable, fussy, and pedantic. He is almost always prosaic. In short, he is a mere human being. In the middle-period dialogues, however—those written after the *Euthydemus*—Socrates has changed. He has become a *theios aner*. He is impossibly brilliant, magnetic, eloquent, and brave. He no longer contents himself with conceptual analysis. The *theios aner* offers images, myths, and symbols, as marvelous as any in the world.[11] What has happened to Socrates?

---

10. For a recent summary of work on the dating of the dialogue, see Thomas Chance, *Plato's Euthydemus: Analysis of What Is and Is Not Philosophy* (Berkeley: University of California Press, 1992). Chance concludes: "In this century, and especially over the last fifty years, there has been an increasing tendency for British and American scholars to fix the position of the Euthydemus as 'late early' or 'early middle.' What this means in practice is that they have now come to place the dialogue before the Meno" (4). Chance would prefer a later dating, in part because he thinks that this will add to the dialogue's importance. I think, on the contrary, that the dialogue gains importance if we view it, as most critics have done, as composed at a time of transition. I think, too, that the content of the dialogue supports "the transitional hypothesis."

11. To see the change in Socrates's character, one has only to compare texts from the early dialogues with middle period texts concerning the same theme. Thus, the aporetic discussion of beauty in the *Hippias Major* may be compared to the mystical portrayal of beauty in the *Phaedrus*; the aporetic discussion of love in the *Lysis* may be compared to the mystical "ascent of love" in the *Symposium*; the perplexity about virtue in all the early dialogues

There are at least two answers to the question. The first answer is that Socrates dies in the *Phaedo* and is reborn a *theios aner*. The second answer is that Socrates "studies" with the brothers, and they make him a *theios aner*. Both answers are true. Socrates undergoes a double initiation. There is the beautiful one in the *Phaedo*, which takes place in the face of death. And there is the nightmare one in the *Euthydemus*, which is bursting with hideous vitality.[12]

---

may be compared to the confident grounding of virtue in a mystical "practice of death" at the start of the *Phaedo*. It is true, on the other band, that the early dialogues of Plato hint at many later doctrines. But the difference in tone and explicitness is, all the same, marked: the early dialogues are inconclusive and mostly conceptual; the middle dialogues are typically poetic and mystical. No doubt, one should not rely on excessively on arguments based upon chronology. The Platonic chronology cannot be known with certainty. Moreover there may be a sense in which Plato worked "all at once" on all the dialogues. His view of unities which grow older and younger than themselves simultaneously (*Parmenides*, 151e–155d) and of "backward-flowing time" under the rule of Cronos (*Statesman*, 271–72) may refer in part to the creative process that he experienced.

12. One could think of other initiators in the dialogues, such as Diotima, the incomparable witch in the *Symposium*, and the dazzling genius Parmenides.

L' Euthydème *n'est pas au nombre de ces dialogues sans lesquels notre image de Platon ne serait pas ce qu'elle est.*

The *Euthydemus* is not among those dialogues without which our image of Plato would not be what it is.

MICHEL NARCY

CHAPTER TWO

The Euthydemus in Previous Commentaries

1. *The Traditional View of Plato's* Euthydemus

The *Euthydemus*, writes Rosamond Kent Sprague, in her well-known work *Plato's Use of Fallacy*, may be viewed as a "scathing satire designed to expose...eristic tricks."[1] That, in brief, is the traditional view of the dialogue.

According to this view, the brothers represent a corrupt strain in philosophy. They do not care about truth or about the future of their pupils. They care only for tricks of debate, and the fees they are paid to perform them. "The two sophists," writes Sprague, "are obviously the villains of the piece, whereas Socrates and Ctesippus are equally obviously the heros."[2] "Eristic," she adds, "...is a joke, but a joke with dangerous pretensions."[3]

The majority of commentators—Gifford, Lamb, Taylor, Guthrie, Friedländer, Findlay, Keulen, Hawtrey, etc.[4]—present a view some-

---

1. Rosamond Kent Sprague, *Plato's Use of Fallacy: A Study of the Euthydemus and Some Other Dialogues* (New York: Barnes & Noble, 1962), xii.
2. Ibid., 12.
3. Ibid., 3.
4. E. H. Gifford, *The Euthydemus of Plato*, with revised text, introduction, notes, and indices (Oxford: Oxford University Press, 1905); *Plato II: Laches, Protagoras, Meno, Euthydemus*, trans. W. R. M. Lamb, Loeb Classical Library 165 (Cambridge: Harvard University Press, 1924); A. E. Taylor, *Plato: The Man and His Work* (London: Methuen and Co. Ltd., 1969); W. K. C. Guthrie, *A History of Greek Philosophy*, vol. 4: Plato: *The Man and His Dialogues—Earlier Period* (London: Cambridge University Press, 1975); Paul Friedländer, *Plato*, vol. 2: *The Dialogues,*

what similar to Sprague's. The brothers are viewed as "the villains;"[5] they give us "clowning"[6] and "mischievous quibbling;"[7] they provide "an entertaining background" against which Socrates can emerge in all his "directness" and "simplicity;"[8] but finally they are "dangerous" and ought, therefore, to be "demolished;"[9] for they might be confused with true and authentic philosophy—and so bring philosophy to ruin.[10] This, then, is the traditional view of the dialogue, a view that emerges in the work of many fine commentators. What will we say of this view? Certainly it is compelling.

Every philosopher at times has the impression that he or she is slipping into nonsense, but the brothers embrace this tendency to nonsense—they take up the cause of nonsense with incredible vehemence and joy. For let there be no mistake, from the point of view of logic, the brothers can only be charlatans. The conjurer, we may say, only seems to hang a rope from the sky. He cannot really do it; the laws of gravity forbid it. The brothers, likewise, cannot really prove themselves omnipotent, or that Socrates is an ox, or that actions never go wrong. If, for a moment, such proofs seem to be given, this can only make us indignant. There must be a trick we can discover.

The brothers, then—precisely because they speak nonsense—arouse our indignation (Plato would say: our *thumos*) and awaken our critical faculties. In truth, the world would collapse if the brothers could prove what they tell us. So we try to discover their

---

First Period, trans. Hans Meyerhoff (New York: Pantheon Books, 1964); J.N. Findlay, *Plato: The Written and Unwritten Doctrines* (New York: Humanities Press, 1974); Hermann Keulen, *Untersuchungen zu Platons "Euthydem"* (Wiesbaden: Otto Harrassowitz, 1971); R.S.W. Hawtrey, *Commentary on Plato's Euthydemus* (Philadelphia: American Philosophical Society, 1981).

5. Sprague, *Plato's Use of Fallacy*, 12.
6. Friedländer, *Plato*, 179.
7. *Plato II*, 375.
8. Taylor, *Plato*, 90.
9. See ibid., 7.
10. In his much admired essay "The Sophists" (*Journal of Philology* 4 [1872]: 288–304), H. Sidgewick explains that an aim of the Euthydemus is to clear up the confusion between the brothers' method and Socrates's.

tricks; we "save the world" in this way. Aristotle, as we know, wrote a handbook of fallacies. It is called, by convention, *The Sophistical Refutations*. But the *Euthydemus*, too, is a kind of "handbook of fallacies." It is a work of logic—though no doubt of an odd sort.[11]

Sprague—who has perhaps aroused more interest in the *Euthydemus* than any other commentator—writes from this point of view. The *Euthydemus*, precisely, exposes eristic tricks, and Sprague's discussion of the brothers' eristic tricks would not be easy to surpass.[12] A similar point of view appears in Hawtrey's helpful commentary.[13] This was the first book-length work on the dialogue to be published in the English language since Gifford's work of 1905.

Recently, a new commentary appeared, that of Thomas Chance (*Plato's Euthydemus: Analysis of What Is and Is Not Philosophy*), and it actually goes further than the others in censuring the brothers:

> Once eristic has been severed from its origins in space and time and transfigured into a symbol, it can be operative whenever and wherever genuine philosophical activity veers from the true path and begins to degenerate into its opposite…
>
> I maintain that in the *Euthydemus* Plato…depicts eristic as the antithesis to dialectic, in fact, as the very paradigm of otherness…

---

11. Hawtrey, among others, elaborates the comparison between the *Euthydemus* and *The Sophistical Refutations*. See his *Commentary*, 22.

12. On Sprague's view of the brothers' style of argument, see 94, n. 6. But equally important is Sprague's demonstration that the eristic tricks to be found in the Euthydemus appear in many other dialogues—where they are refined, toned down, and employed by Socrates himself. Now, certainly Plato recognized the fallacious nature of these arguments. It was he, after all, who exposed them in the *Euthydemus*. But it remains a somewhat vexing question why the *Cratylus*, the *Meno*, the *Thaetetus*, etc. should exhibit (in the person of Socrates) a mode of disputation that Plato himself, in a previous dialogue, had satirized and thoroughly discredited. See her *Plato's Use of Fallacy*, 43.

13. Hawtrey has collated the work of many previous critics of the *Euthydemus*—a help to anyone working on this text.

Unleashing all the forces of his tragic and comic art, his powers of persuasion and dissuasion, his love of irony and satire, and even an impulse to slander and abuse, Plato has created for our inspection that measure of baseness and ugliness in all philosophy, and thereby transformed the brothers into types from which we are to turn. (19)

In the course of his book, Chance describes how the brothers careen between a "bogus esotericism" based on "ambiguity"[14] and a narrow "logical-linguistic analysis."[15] They represent what Plato disliked about his intellectual epoch, and also (since Plato has made them into archetypes) they seem to reflect what troubles us about philosophy in our time. Chance expresses well the enormity of the brothers, the vastness of what they stand for—though he recoils from them and finds no good in them.

Before going on to discuss a second set of commentators, I would like to recall from Chapter One those aspects of the *Euthydemus* that, taken together, cannot be explained within the framework of a satire on eristic: the odd passivity of Socrates, the fantastic applause bestowed upon the brothers, the presentation by the brothers of certain cherished doctrines of Plato (pre-existence, recollection, etc.); and above all the shocking images and thoughts that recur in the brothers' discourse: desecration, murder, and human sacrifice.[16]

---

14. Thomas Chance, *Plato's Euthydemus: Analysis of What Is and Is Not Philosophy* (Berkeley: University of California Press, 1992), 110.

15. Ibid., 51.

16. In his foreword to W. B. Stanford's *The Ulysses Theme* (Thompson, Conn.: Spring Publications, 2022), Charles Boer calls attention to the "civilized" or "gentlemanly" comportment of many classical scholars that required them to ignore, or tone down, or "leave to others...to explore" much that is strange in classical literature. "Be careful of the smooth-talking Professor Stanford," Boer writes, "as you take this little break for tea, or he will charm you into swallowing the wildest poison!" (xi).

2. *New Light on the* Euthydemus

I must now speak briefly of three interesting commentaries that break, to some extent, with the traditional view of the dialogue: Leo Strauss's "On the Euthydemus,"[17] Michel Narcy's *Le Philosophe et son double*,[18] and Monique Canto's *L'Intrigue philosophique*.[19] In all three commentaries, the point of departure is this. Socrates, we are told, does not win his fight against the brothers. We think he is going to win, because usually he is invincible. We want him to win, because he is far more attractive than they are. Yet the victory of Socrates—the victory we anticipate so confidently—never actually occurs. What is it, then, that happens?

Perhaps, as Narcy thinks, it is Socrates who is defeated,[20] or perhaps, as Canto has it, the contest ends in an ambiguous manner and there are no winners at all. Another possibility—implied by Strauss—is that Socrates does not even want to prevail against the brothers, because secretly he likes them and in some way believes in their cause. It is Socrates, after all, who invites the brothers to speak, who "lends himself" to their performance (305a), who causes his own exhortations to fail and "redound" in their favor, who loudly applauds them, who defends them when Crito attacks them. These are evident signs of complicity.[21]

And yet—what does this mean? Why this lack of victory for Socrates? If Plato wishes to show us that Socrates cannot beat the brothers (or secretly sides with the brothers), there must be something admirable in the brothers (as Socrates himself insists in several places—288b, 278c). We ought to state what this admirable element would be. Here again, several views are offered to us.

---

17. Leo Strauss, "On the Euthydemus," *Interpretation* 1, no. 1 (1970): 14.
18. Michel Narcy, *Le Philosophe et son double: Un commentaire de l'Euthydème de Plato* (Paris: J. Vrin, 1984), 8.
19. Monique Canto, *L'Intrigue philosophique: Essai sur l'Euthydème de Platon* (Paris: Société d'Édition "Les Belles Lettres," 1987), 231
20. Narcy, *Le Philosophe et son double*, 8.
21. Strauss, "On the Euthydemus," 14.

According to Monique Canto, the admirable thing about the brothers is their "constructive" way of thinking; their confident way of choosing philosophic positions and then shrewdly manipulating words, forcing words to "validate" their views. Plato, Canto thinks, appreciates this—which in any case represents an important trend in philosophy. Plato, indeed, has been influenced by this, for he himself will turn increasingly to constructive or systematic writing, and he hopes to infuse the love and authenticity of Socrates into this new, more constructive, mode of thought.[22]

Narcy's view is rather different. According to Narcy, the virtue of the brothers is their "will to power" or competitiveness. They do not care about truth (love of truth is the downfall of Socrates). They care only for victory in contests, and the less "true" their position, the more stunning their victory will seem. Plato, however, admires the brothers, and in general he admires the aims and methods of eristics. Plato's work may be viewed as a celebration of eristic battles, because truth emerges only in a conflict between perspectives, and the conflict will be liveliest when personal victory is the prize.[23]

Strauss's view, again, is different from Narcy's and Canto's. According to Strauss, the virtue of the brothers is that they stand opposed to the "border person" who appears in the closing pages of the dialogue (304e) and who requires of philosophy that it merge with political activity, on pain of becoming frivolous. Socrates, as we learn in the *Apology* (31d), consistently refuses to engage in political activity and prefers, we may assume, the risk of becoming frivolous. But the brothers, too, accept the risk of being frivolous (as their exhibition demonstrates). Socrates thus promotes their cause.[24]

---

22. The *Euthydemus*, for Canto, reveals "a new condition of thought"—a condition "which brings it about that the quest [for wisdom] is no longer the place of a maze, a drama, or a struggle, but rather the place of positivity, without irony or intrigue, without the play of otherness," *L'Intrigue philosophique*, 242.

23. Narcy, *Le Philosophe et son double*, 141–44.

24. It seems to Strauss that, at the end of the dialogue, "Socrates has successfully vindicated Euthydemus and what he stands for," "On the Euthydemus," 20.

Such then, briefly, are the "revisionist" commentaries of Strauss, Narcy, and Canto. Yet, I have not done justice to, for example, the peculiar "suggestiveness" of Strauss, or to Narcy's fine discussion of "the rules of eristic" and the "slipperiness" of irony, or to Canto's evocation of a restless, empty, errant love of wisdom (i.e. Socrates's love) making room for a "technology of words." I think, however, that anyone reading these commentaries will want to question, at least to a point, the traditional view of the dialogue—that the brothers are merely the "villains" and are thoroughly "demolished" at last.

Yet I cannot shake the feeling that the most important thing—the most bewildering and obvious thing about the dialogue—is still neglected, though in view of the brothers' "rehabilitation," it has become more obtrusive than before. I am thinking of the content of the brothers' exhibition—the murdered youths, the severed heads, and so on. Strauss, Narcy, and Canto glide over this content rather lightly, as if they were somehow expecting it but feel no need to discuss it. Erists, they tell us, are supposed to say strange things. Yes, but why these things? Why not others, less appalling?

3. *The* Euthydemus *and the History of Religion*

My view of the dialogue is that the content of the brothers' discourse is of the highest importance, and that the brothers represent a kind of "dream condensation" of two distinct figures—the sophist and the Corybantic dancer. Thus, the form of the brothers' discourse may be called "sophistical," but the content of the discourse—the shocking scenarios and images—may be traced to the Corybantic rites (or similar ecstatic rites), as Socrates seems to see:

> Do not be surprised, my dear Cleinias, if the arguments of our visitors seem strange to you, for perhaps you do not see what they are doing to you. They are acting like the celebrants of the Corybantic rites, when they perform the chairing...(277d)

Thus, the history of religion provides a key to the brothers' discourse.

The view of Plato that emerges in my study is related to the view that develops in such writers as E.R. Dodds,[25] Mircea Eliade,[26] Francis Cornford,[27] W.K.C. Guthrie,[28] David Tracy,[29] I.P. Couliano,[30] and others. According to this view, Plato stands at the crossroad of archaic and modern experience. He is "modern" in the sense that he participates in the so-called "Sophistic Enlightenment," which is the earliest emergence of a familiar style of thought—ironic, reflective, skeptical, rational, progressive. But at the same time he is drawn to "archaic" modes of experience, which still form the substrate of Greek civilized life—to shamanistic journeys and Dionysian mania, to "cyclical time" and timeless "archetypal" modes of being, to an "intimacy with the world" which makes the world "epiphanic"—one could extend this list.[31]

But I feel sure the writers cited in the previous paragraph would ask us to proceed with caution. The "archaic" and "modern" elements in Greek civilization are hard to disentangle, and simple concepts and schemata, employed in an "objectifying" manner, provide at best a provisional clarity. We should thus plunge into a text—a text like the *Euthydemus*, with all its specificity.

This much, however, I want to suggest at the outset. I think that Plato's secret—the secret of his power—is that he is a figure at the crossroads. While he has appropriated a "modern" way of think-

---

25. E.R. Dodds, *The Greeks and the Irrational* (Berkeley: University of California Press, 1971).

26. Eliade's references to Plato are scattered over many volumes, but see, for example, "Mythologies of Memory and Forgetting," in *Myth and Reality*, trans. Willard R. Trask (New York: Harper and Row, 1963), and the first chapter of *Cosmos and History*, trans. Willard R. Trask (New York: Harper Torchbooks, 1959).

27. F.M. Cornford, *From Religion to Philosophy: A Study in the Origins of Western Speculation* (New York: Harper Torchbooks, 1957).

28. W.K.C. Guthrie, *The Greeks and Their Gods* (Boston: Beacon Press, 1955).

29. David Tracy, lectures delivered at the University of Chicago, Winter, 1987.

30. I.P. Couliano, *Out of This World: Otherworldly Journeys from Gilgamesh to Albert Einstein* (Boston: Shambhala, 1991), 114–54.

31. See, for example, the text of Dodds and Eliade cited above.

ing (skeptical, rational, hyper-reflective, and so on), he remains in touch with the archaic past, including modes of experience largely suppressed for millennia. The discourse of the brothers—with its "modern" sophistical form and its wild "Corybantic" content—may serve as an image (distorted as in a dream) of Plato's own experience.

I am saying, in effect, that the brothers are Plato—an outrageous, diabolical, most brutally "bifurcated" Plato. They teach Plato's doctrines to Socrates—to ironic, skeptical, eternally "modern" Socrates. And, he grows "young and beautiful" again.

4. The Plan of this Book

The *Euthydemus*, as has been noted, is a drama in five acts, of which the first, third, and fifth are exhibitions by the brothers, and the second and fourth are exhortations to philosophy by Socrates. I devote a chapter to each part of the drama—five chapters in all. It seems best, however, to begin with the chapters on Socrates, and then proceed to the brothers. Socrates is a familiar figure; he can help us get our bearings.

After the chapters on the five parts of the dialogue, I offer, in conclusion, some brief comments on Pindar's first Olympian ode. The last words of Socrates to the brothers allude to this ode, which is perhaps Pindar's greatest. The opening lines of the ode (the part cited by Socrates) are: "Best of all things is water; but gold, like a gleaming fire, by night outshines all pride of wealth beside."[32] These lines, I think, sum up the meaning of the *Euthydemus* and perhaps, too, hold some key to all of Plato's work.

---

32. *The Odes of Pindar*, trans. Richard Lattimore (Chicago: University of Chicago Press, 1970).

The stick digs the ground in order to ensure the growth of a plant; the plant is cultivated in order to be eaten; it is eaten in order to maintain the life of the one who cultivates it...The absurdity of an endless deferral only justifies the equivalent absurdity of a true end, which would itself serve no purpose. What a "true end" introduces is the continuous being, lost in the world as water is lost in water...

GEORGE BATAILLE, *Theory of Religion*

CHAPTER THREE
The First Socratic Discourse

We have to begin with the Socratic discourses because they raise the question to which the brothers provide an answer, or to be more precise, because they reveal the state of mind—the Socratic state of mind—which the brothers overcome with their rites.

In saying this, I am only repeating what Socrates says to the Brothers: "For my part, I shall see if I can rouse them, making them pity my eagerness and seriousness, and so be serious themselves...Let us beg them and extort them to shine for us" (288c), and again: "In my eagerness to listen to your wisdom, I dare to improvise in your presence..." (278d–e). Socrates, of course, is being ironic here. But though an ironic statement "means" the opposite of what it "says," it often (notoriously) also means what it says. That is the case here.[1]

Better yet, however, one interprets the tone of Socrates's utterances, it is certainly the case that, when Socrates speaks with Cleinias, he rushes quite self-consciously into the sort of trap that the brothers can help him escape. When Socrates reaches the point where he "bellows" for the brothers (293a), he has fulfilled the aim of his discourse and is calling for the help he needs.[2]

---

1. I cannot help thinking here of Narcy's view of irony—that it is a kind of "evasiveness" or "slipperiness." It is comparable to the oil that wrestlers put on to let slip their opponent's grip (*Le Philosophe et son double*, 41).

2. Few commentators even consider this possibility—that the "help" the brothers provide is the sort that Socrates requires. It is true that Narcy con-

1. *Having It All*

> We all want to do well, Cleinias, I said, but how can we do well? Will we do well, do you think, if good things are present with us? (279a)

Socrates, having raised this question, goes on to paint a portrait of what many people, perhaps, are tempted to view as the ideal. The ideal is "having it all;" materially and spiritually.

Imagine a person—let us say a man—who has all good things at his disposal. What would this man have? Socrates and Cleinias make up a kind of list. He would have the goods of the body: beauty, agility, wealth, and health. He would have the goods that satisfy the ego (Plato would say the "thumotic" goods): fame, honor, and the admiration of all who know him. He would have, finally, the more rarified goods of the soul (temperance, justice, courage, and wisdom). Socrates and Cleinias agree after reflection that these things, too, are worth having (279a–d). So we can imagine our ideal man. Beautifully barbered and clothed, he arrives in his carriage at his place of work where, with the approval of all who love him, he works for the good of humanity.

Nothing is denied to this man. He rejoices in wisdom and justice. He rejoices in beauty, fame, and wealth. Does he lack anything at all? Can unhappiness arise within this fullness of possession?

We might wish to reply that between the different possessions tensions are sure to arise. Thus, the justice present in this man will prevent him from keeping his wealth. The temperance present in this man will prevent him from using his beauty to procure sexual pleasure. The wisdom present in this man will prevent him from taking seriously the crowd's approbation, and we could go on in this vein. But this is not what Socrates says. He wants us to dream of a paradise of presence, and its content is less important, at the moment, than the sheer fact of its plenitude. Let us suppose, con-

---

siders it, but his view is the opposite of mine. The brothers, according to Narcy, evade giving Socrates the help for which he asks (or evade frankly admitting that they do not know how to give it). This evasion is a part of their triumph (*Le Philosophe et son double*, 56).

sequently, that paradise is really Paradise—that the good things listed fit together in it. Would anything, then, be missing?

What is missing is the greatest good of all.

2. *Good Fortune*

> By heaven, Cleinias, I said recollecting, we very nearly forgot the greatest good of all.
>
> What's that? he asked.
>
> Good fortune, I answered. (279c)

"Good fortune" is of course the greatest good. Suppose that in some miraculous manner, we are invited to fulfill the ideal that Socrates and Cleinias somewhat humorously unfold for us. We have only to say the word and some vast and curious power will give us beauty, wealth, health, adoration, and will also, if we wish, make us "good." There is only one difficulty. If we decide to accept these benefits, we must give up our luck in return. In a stroke, we receive everything—but our luck is altogether gone. Henceforth, life will go badly for us.

Would anyone take this offer? Presumably no one would take it. The greatest goods in the world are worth nothing without luck, for one requires luck to keep them. If the future is doomed and we know it, the present moment seems unhappy to us, and the richer it is, the more unhappy it makes us, for it taunts us with what we will lose.

Everything Socrates says in his exhortation depends upon this: that humans (by nature?) are preoccupied with the future. The present rises before us, but we withdraw and form pictures of the future: on these pictures, our happiness depends. And now that Socrates has displayed the plenitude of goods and has made them depend on good fortune, he has only to show that wisdom guarantees good fortune, and Cleinias will seek wisdom more eagerly than any other good.

3. *Wisdom*

> But we are making ourselves ridiculous, Cleinias, I said.
>
> What's wrong now? he said.
>
> Wisdom, I replied, is the same thing as good fortune, as any child can see. (279d)

How does Socrates prove that wisdom is the same as good fortune?[3] He begins by pointing out that those who are wisest at flute-playing fare best when they play the flute. And those who are wisest at soldiering and sailing fare best at war and at sea. And those who are wisest at doctoring fare best when treating disease (279e). Certainly, there are times when wisdom shapes the future the way craftsmen shape the material they use, and then wisdom and good fortune are the same.

But just as Socrates is about to speak of those other cases where bad fortune overwhelms human wisdom (as when an unconquerable tempest defeats the wisest sailor, or overwhelming numbers defeat the wisest soldier, or when, to speak with Thucydides, the wisest doctors are the first to die of the plague, because they are the first exposed to it); at just that point, when fragile human wisdom is about to encounter the powers that destroy it and take control of the future away from it—at that point a kind of "dream censorship" descends, and the dialogue is temporarily blurred (280b).

---

3. Socrates's exhortation—and especially 279d—acquires special meaning in the light of Martha C. Nussbaum's *The Fragility of Goodness: Luck and Ethics in Greek Tragedy and Philosophy* (Cambridge: Cambridge University Press, 1986). Nussbaum, it is true, does not speak of the passage in question, but the great theme of her book is "the aspiration to rational self-sufficiency in Greek ethical thought." She shows how Plato, who embodied this tendency, aspired to create through "the controlling power of reason," a mode of human life entirely "safe from luck (3)." We may say, that 279d of the *Euthydemus*—where wisdom and luck are declared to be identical—expresses the program that, according to Nussbaum, is a central theme of Plato's work. Nussbaum, on the other hand, shows adroitly how Plato is ambivalent with regard to his own program. The *Euthydemus*, too, expresses this ambivalence—for example, at 280b, where Socrates's triumphant argument concerning luck is amusingly "censored" or suppressed.

For the dialogue, as we know, takes the form of a story that Socrates tells to his old friend Crito. And at just this point, where so much appears to be at stake, and so many objections must have occurred to all who listened, Socrates decides that the discussion is not worth repeating and sums it up in a few lines. However, he assures us that his argument was successful and everyone came over to his side.

But what did Socrates say? That is the point—nobody knows. Reporting the argument to Crito, Socrates compresses it into such a narrow space that neither Crito nor anyone else could possibly make much sense of it. The only remark preserved is that "wisdom couldn't err...if she did, she wouldn't be wisdom"—and "on this we somehow agreed, how I do not know" (280b).[4] What, then, is the moral?

We began in a paradise of presence—a material and spiritual paradise. We "fell" out of anxiety for when the future started to frighten us, the present no longer made us happy. At that point, Socrates came forward and assured us that our anxiety was unnecessary because wisdom masters the future the way flute players master the flute. Socrates proved this, too, but somehow the proof was censored.

This much, at least, is clear. Wisdom, driven by anxiety, detaches itself from presence and looks for a way to master it. And so the dream of "having it all" vanishes away, and we confront a world of mere utility.

---

4. But what could the argument have been? And would Plato himself have accepted it? If we take the realm of fortune to be that of the goddess Ananke (Necessity), it must be said that not even God (the demiurge of the *Timaeus*) can completely conquer Ananke—and this, according to Plato, is why there are many flaws in the world (30a, 48a). In the same way, the wise philosopher-rulers presented in the *Republic* are helpless to save their state from ruin (546d); and the enlightened hero who returns to the cave is quickly sacrificed to vicious, irrational powers (517a). Then in what sense can wisdom replace fortune? It seems to me that—much as Plato desired it otherwise—he was obliged to conclude that wisdom could replace fortune only in the sense that Socrates, dying—apparently crushed by his enemies—remained, in a way, the most fortunate person of all since an eternity of splendor lay before him (58e).

4. *Utility, Darkness, Slavery*

> Will we be happy, Cleinias, in the presence of good things, if they don't give us profit, or if they do give us profit?
>
> If they do give us profit.
>
> And would a thing give us profit if it were merely present to us, if we made no use of it?
>
> Of course not. (280*b–c*)

What follows from this is one of the most agreeable and whimsical arguments in all Platonism. But it is also an argument that troubles us, because it expresses a state of mind in which happiness is impossible, as Socrates knows.

He begins by pointing out that things make us happy only if they give us a profit, and mere presence, of course, is unprofitable. To profit from things requires use. His examples are quite entertaining.

Suppose, he says, we have a most distinguished wine—but no one drinks it. Will that be profitable? Obviously not. And suppose we have a most delicious dinner, cooked by the finest chef, but we let it grow cold and no one eats it. Will that be profitable? Obviously not. Suppose, finally, that all the craftsmen in the world are given perfectly apportioned workrooms furnished with the most exquisite tools—but the craftsmen, declining to work, make no use of the workrooms or tools—will these, then, be profitable? Again, the answer is no (280*c*).

Only a moment ago, we decided that presence counted for little, since the future was the greatest good of all. Thus presence appears as that which needs to be used, as we give the future its shape. The wine, the dinner, the workroom, the tools—lying about unused, they seem, as Socrates shows, to be excessive, opaque, absurd, for it is only in use that they have meaning for us. It is their use that gives them their worth.

But now we reach the point where the enigmatic Socrates makes his position somewhat bizarre. The apparently natural admission that things, unused, are altogether unprofitable, is quickly going to cause Cleinias to renounce all that he is and plunge recklessly into the the dark, the dull, the dim. How does this come about?

Socrates first gets Cleinias to agree that the paradise they designed for themselves at the start of their conversation will be useless to them unless it is used by them, for there is no happiness from things apart from use. This use, moreover, must be right use; and right use, precisely, is use guided by *sophia*—that is, guided by wisdom or skill (280d–e).

Here, then, for the second time in our discourse, wisdom extracts us from the present by its promise to dominate the future; but for the ever-ironic Socrates, darkness is looming up close. Let us watch as it swallows Cleinias.

> Then can we, in heaven's name, get any profit from our possessions without understanding and wisdom? Consider, if you will, Cleinias, the case of a man who does and possesses much but who is entirely lacking in intelligence—will he really be better off than if he did and possessed little? Look at it like this. Wouldn't he err less, if he did less? And erring less, do less ill? And doing less ill, be less wretched?
>
> Yes.
>
> In which case will one do less—when one is poor or when one is rich?
>
> When one is poor.
>
> And when one is weak or when one is strong?
>
> Weak.
>
> And when one is brave and self-controlled...or when one is a coward?
>
> A coward.
>
> And when idle rather than busy?
>
> Yes.
>
> And slow rather than quick? And with sight and hearing that are dim (*amblus*) rather than sharp?
>
> He agreed to these and all such cases. (281b–d)

I sometimes think that this text—which is whimsical, ironic, enchantingly repetitive, and ends with the plunge into dim dullness (the *amblus*)—reveals the essence of Socratic discourse. What happens, then, in this text?

Cleinias agrees to renounce his wealth, his health, his courage, his light and his life, if he cannot find the secret of using these things rightly. Of course, he cannot find the secret for as Socrates will show in his second exhortation, the secret is not to be found. But Cleinias, for the moment, remains unaware of the implications of his agreement, and Socrates sums up as follows:

> It seems, then, Cleinias, I proceeded, that as regards all those things which at first we declared good, the main question about them is not how they are good in themselves, but rather, I would say, the point is this. If these things are guided by ignorance, they are greater evils than their opposite, insofar as they can minister (*hyperetein*) to the needs of their evil guide; whereas if understanding and wisdom guide them, they are greater goods; but in themselves, either way, they're worth—nothing.[5] (281d)

We are asked to imagine a world in which all good things "are more evil than good," because all things are ruled by misuse. Brightness misused is worse than darkness; courage misused is worse than cowardice; beauty misused is worse than ugliness, etc. Thus presence, which was first subordinated to the future, is now revealed as a neutral mass. It gains value only when it "ministers" to the wisdom that guides right use.

Finally, Socrates says:

> If a man thinks (as well he may) that it is necessary to procure this from his father more than money, and from his guardians and ordinary friends, and from those who profess to be his lovers, whether strangers or fellow citizens,

---

5. Alcibiades—doomed former pupil of Socrates and relation to Cleinias (275*b*)—seems to be in question in this passage. "Alcibiades," comments Canto, "is the very model of a gifted nature, destroyed by lack of education"—destroyed by a lack of that wisdom which would teach him how to use his gifts; the wisdom of which Socrates is speaking (*L'Intrigue philosophique*, 118).

and if he prays and beseeches them to give him his share of wisdom—there is nothing shameful in this, Cleinias, or in any way deserving of reproach, if, for the sake of wisdom, he becomes a slave and ministers to a lover or any other man, and is ready to minister (*hyperetein*) in any honorable manner in his eagerness to be wise. Is not this your view?

Most certainly that is my view. (282*b*)

The principle of domination, whereby all that is present and actual "ministers" to wisdom, reappears here, as the youth "ministers" (same word) to the teacher of wisdom—enslaving himself and ministering "in any honorable manner." On that peculiar note—with Cleinias a slave—the first Socratic exhortation ends. The liberation of Cleinias follows.

HAMLET: The King is a thing...
ROSENCRANTZ: A thing, my Lord?
HAMLET: Of nothing...

                         WILLIAM SHAKESPEARE

CHAPTER FOUR

The Second Socratic Discourse

1. *Paradise Regained*

> Now, what knowledge must we acquire if we acquire knowledge rightly? Is it not simply knowledge that will profit us? (298e)

Here we begin the second Socratic exhortation. Everything that is—all material and spiritual presence—has been subordinated to wisdom, which knows how to use things skillfully. All things should "minister" to wisdom. But what sort of wisdom are we seeking? Obviously, a profitable sort of wisdom, the most profitable sort of all.

We now allow our minds to wander a little, in order to gain an insight into this "most profitable" wisdom. How will we know it when we see it? What marks—if any—will distinguish it?

Let us suppose, Socrates says, that we knew how to find the place "where the earth has the most gold buried in it" (288e). Or better yet, let us suppose that, without the slightest exertion, we "got all the gold in the world" or that "we knew how to turn mere stones into gold" (289a).[1] Would that profit us?

Everyone knows the answer to that question, and everyone, I suppose, likes to answer it, too. We dream of boundless gold, and we feel a kind of thrill. Then it occurs to us that the gold is going to

---

1. "The wish that has fathered alchemy," writes Hawtrey, "has had a long history!" (*Commentary*, 121).

help us only if we use it wisely; it will hurt us if badly used. Next, we have bad dreams. Corrupted by the wealth which we did not know how to handle, we sink irremediably into dissolution and lethargy. Finally, we wake up—how good it is to be poor! Now, the pleasure here is that of a double transcendence, since first we get beyond poverty, and then we get beyond wealth. We finish—this time happily—where we began.

Assuredly more poignant is the fantasy about immortality. Suppose, Socrates asks, that we knew how to make ourselves immortal—"would that profit us" (289*b*)? It would profit us, Socrates warns, in one case only—if we knew how to use our boundless life. And so, in our fantasy, we are released from the fear of dying, but only to be punished (as Sisyphus and Tantalus were punished) by a suffering which is limitless, since it has no limit in death. Here, as with the gold, we return to our point of departure: if indeed we are capable of dying, we are perhaps better off as we are.

We can see what Socrates is doing. At the start of his first exhortation, he asked us to envision what was really a kind of paradise, since everything we desired—all material and spiritual wealth—was set before us as our own. But anxiety ruined this paradise. We were nervous about "good fortune." Then, in place of paradise, we confronted a world of ends and means, after which we plunged into the dark, the dull.

Now we are listening to the second exhortation, which begins by reversing the first. Fulfilling the alchemist's dream, we make ourselves immortal and turn the world to gold. We create, by our own hand, a paradise more excellent than the paradise which we lost. All this happens through knowledge—that is, through technology or art. Thus, the Greek word *techne* (which we translate here as "art") starts to recur in the exhortation.

But will this paradise made by our art retrieve our vanished happiness? We can already see that it will not retrieve our happiness. The fact that we can make paradise does not insure we can use it. It could certainly bring us to harm. An eternity of splendor comes within our grasp—but we, about to reach out for it, immediately put ourselves "beyond" it for we are haunted by the image of the future to which it will lead (289*b*).

What, then, do we want? "The sort of knowledge we require, fair youth, is that in which we find, at one and the same time, an art of making and of using the thing made" (289*b*). This apparently modest formula conceals an abyss of thought. Socrates has noticed that, whenever happiness comes to us, we leap "beyond" it, pursuing its use. It seems we will never be happy. If, in spite of this, there is an art which makes happiness possible for us, it must be an art which is itself already beyond that which it puts before us, and which has used what it gives in advance.

Absurd images occur to us in this connection. One sews a coat—by wearing it. One makes a lyre—by playing it. One cooks a meal—by eating it. But such is the art of happiness, if the art of happiness exists. Now, what particular art would this be?

2. *A Superior Power*

Somewhat comically, Socrates proposes that the art of happiness might be that of the speech-maker or general. The speech-maker and the general are both figures of authority. And we may say (speaking roughly), that the speech-maker persuades; and when the speech-maker's views are accepted, the general imposes them by force.

Neither the speech-maker nor the general particularly tempt Cleinias. The speech-maker, Cleinias argues, insofar as he is a maker (in contrast to a reader or performer) does not use the speeches he makes but makes them for other agencies, on whose skill their effect depends. The general, likewise, does not use the cities he conquers but delivers them to statesmen, whose task is to draw a profit from them (289*d*).

All that is clear enough—but do we notice anything strange about the pages under discussion? Strange figures, surely, appear as illustrations in them. The speech-maker is compared to a charmer of beasts; the general is compared to a hunter of beasts. Astronomers, geometers, and calculators are said to be hunters of realities. These three figures, we are told, are to the dialectician what the general is to the statesman and the hunter is to the cook (289d–290c).[2]

Much could be said about the significance of these figures, but Plato, I think, intends to be mysterious, and his ultimate meaning is at this point rather obscure. What is obvious, on the other hand, is that Socrates has made two rather naive suggestions concerning the art of happiness, and these have been dealt with by Cleinias in a surprisingly sophisticated way. In fact, one of Cleinias's speeches—his speech at 290b, which is his last speech in the dialogue—astonishes us with its brilliance, and it also astonishes Crito, to whom Socrates is "telling" the conversation.

> What is this, Socrates? Such words from that stripling?
>
> You do not believe it, Crito?
>
> I should rather think not. (290e)

And what about us? Do we believe it? Did Cleinias "really" make the speech at 290b with its vast range of reference and its brilliant, sardonic analogies? And if not Cleinias, who?

> I wonder if possibly Ctessipus made the speech, and somehow it slipped from my mind.
>
> Ctesippus? Never!
>
> Well, at any rate, Crito, at least I can tell you this: Euthydemus didn't make it, and neither did Dionysodorus. (290e)

And what about us? Are we sure the brothers didn't make it? As a matter of fact, it is obviously rather foolish to ask which of the

---

2. Leo Strauss's interpretation of the Euthydemus places much stress on this passage. According to Strauss, Cleinias's reply to Socrates (though undoubtedly brilliant) incorporates an error encouraged by Socrates himself, since Cleinias would prevent the art of dialectic (an art that has no product) from assuming the place of "Royal Art." Thus, according to Strauss, "the whole exhortation cannot but redound to the benefit of eristic;" and Socrates, somewhat humorously, has intentionally advanced the brothers' cause ("On the *Euthydemus*," 14).

speakers "really" made the speech. The question has no answer. The whole dialogue is—untrue.³

> But then, heaven help me! Tell me, mysterious Crito, was it some superior power that spoke that speech? For that speech I heard, I am sure. (291a)

In this way it comes home to us that all the voices in the dialogue arise from the voice of Socrates speaking with Crito, and that Socrates's voice and Crito's emanate from a certain superior power which cannot be named within the dialogue.

As for the art of happiness, Socrates and Cleinias search for it for a long time. Socrates, as he recounts the dialogue, compresses the discussion, just as, on an earlier occasion, he compressed the discussion of the identity of wisdom and luck. "What need to tell the story at length?" he asks (291b).

However it is clear that Socrates and Cleinias considered many arts. But the art they sought eluded them the way larks elude children who chase them (291b). The conversation ended with the kingly art—the most splendid and deceptive of all.

3. The King

When we reached the kingly art, we felt sure it was what we were seeking. We thought that it caused right conduct in the state, and that, as we read in Aeschylus:

---

3. Because Socrates raises the question that the brothers attempt to answer, I wanted to discuss the two Socratic exhortations before turning to the brothers' performance. However, it is true that, as a result of this procedure, I have not been able to emphasize certain structural features of the dialogue. Consider, for example, the text at 290e—where Crito protests that Cleinias simply could not have made the remarks that Socrates has ascribed to him. We find ourselves here more or less at the center of the dialogue, at the very heart of the central conversation. Canto remarks that, from this point forward, "Criton ne croit plus au recit de Socrate" (*L'Intrigue philosophique*, 160), and this is of the highest importance. It seems that, at the center of the text, the reality of the text is denied from within the text, so the dreamlike or quasi-hallucinatory quality that the text was meant to possess is in this way acknowledged by Plato.

> It sits by itself
> At the helm of the city
> Steering the whole,
> Commanding the whole,
> conferring a use on all beings. (291*d*)

The King now appears—a remote, contracted purposefulness. We are looking for the art of happiness—is that not the art of Kings?

All arts "hand over" their products to the King, who alone knows how to use them. That is to say, all production in the city, all products of making and hunting, are incomplete or deficient, because they cannot, through their own agency, control their future use. But the King controls just this.

For example, this sentence I am writing is deficient to the degree that it cannot, on its own, assure its "use" in my book. And if my book ever appears, it, too, will be deficient, because it cannot, in itself, guarantee that readers will read it or read it with any profit. Knowing this, I am nervous—no sentence reassures me. My book will not really satisfy me. However, the King's art would fix all that—"steering the whole, commanding the whole, conferring a use on all beings" (291*d*).

At this point—as in all such discussions—the image of a ship "rises" to the surface. The ship is tossed by rushing water, and the ship is the city, and the monarch-captain sits alone at the helm. All future right use, all goodness not yet actual, is compressed in a single point. "But does the King's art, ruling over all, produce anything" (291*b*)? To be sure, the King is the point but what is the point of the point?

Someone will say that the point does not need a point—and that is the special charm of the point. But that is not true in this case, because we are working on the premise that the art of the King is the art of promoting happiness. Now, the King does not make us happy merely by being the King. The King, consequently, must produce the thing that makes us happy, and we want to know what this is.

To answer the question, Socrates imagines an admirable King. He rules for the sake of the people, and he succeeds in doing all that a king can do. He makes everyone wealthy and free and makes peace pervade the land. Will this achievement guarantee our happiness?

How can it guarantee our happiness? It is perfectly possible to be rich, free, at peace with one's neighbors and miserable. Everything depends on the use we make of what we have. What, then, do we want from the King? "Nothing," it seems, "can be good but some sort of knowledge"—the King will teach us to use what we have (292*b*). Yet as soon as we say this, the King disappears like a ghost. He leaves nothing behind but the vacuous notion of rightness, and this is where we began.[4]

> When we examined the art of Kings, we found we were in a maze...We thought we had reached the end, but the maze turned again, and we found ourselves back at the beginning, as much in want as before. (291*b*)

Now we collapse into a delirium of repetition as an empty good, descending from the King to others and yet others, gradually spreads out everywhere, until the whole earth is suffused with it. For the King is useful and good. This can only mean that he makes others useful and good:

---

4. As Rosamund Kent Sprague has shown in *Plato's Philosopher-King: A Study of the Theoretical Background* (Columbia: University of South Carolina Press, 1976), the sort of thing that happens at 292*d* in the *Euthydemus* has happened before in Plato and will happen again in later dialogues. Each time it happens—each time, that is to say, the art that ought to be highest turns out to be vacuous—a peculiar pattern emerges, which Sprague has described in detail. Elements in the pattern include "paradox," "reflectivity," questions of usefulness and useless "*tinos* words," and "regressions" (see 48–56). There is something about the pattern—the way it always emerges under certain specific conditions—that seems odd to the point of eeriness. Here we draw close to Plato's deepest concerns—concerns about a pattern in which the "highest" is proved to be vacuous. Now, as Sprague has shown in her book, Plato's solution to the difficulty is given in the *Republic*; it is the philosopher-ruler. But I want to stress that the philosopher-ruler is a mystic and that his capacity is based upon mystical insight. The philosopher-ruler has seen that which is highest (the Idea of the Good) and thus knows—simply knows—that the highest is not vacuous, because all value and fullness flow out of it.

> And how are they useful and good? Shall we not venture to say that they are to make others so, and these again others? In what way they are good remains unknown. It is merely a case of the proverbial Corinthus son of Zeus (*ho dios Korinthos*). (292*d*)

But who or what is the proverbial *ho dios Korinthos*?

4. Ho Dios Korinthos

> ...To say this thrice and four times over turns into futility, like the meaningless cry among children—*ho dios Korinthos*.[5]

Ho dios Korinthos (Corinthus son of Zeus) was a yell of children. This much we know from Pindar, but we cannot be absolutely certain how the yell was used. The main thing is that the words were chanted over and over again, and they were probably chanted as a kind of mocking echo of a person or a power who was threatening yet ineffectual, a bit like the cry of our own children—"nya, na, na, NA, na! You can't CATCH me!"

Here is the story of the cry *ho dios Korinthos*. It is told by the scholist on Pindar, and it is confirmed by the scholist on Aristophanes,[6] who also speaks of the cry.

Long ago, the island of Megara belonged to Corinth, but the day came when the Megarians desired and demanded their liberty. The Corinthians dispatched a spokesman who talked in the grand manner saying, "You do not honor *ho dios Korinthos*, verily, *ho dios Korinthos* is grieved at your conduct," and so on, with the perpetual introduction of the phrase *ho dios Korinthos*. Finally, the Megarians lost all patience and set upon the speaker. Taking up the motto of *ho dios Korinthos*, they proceeded to defeat the Corinthian troops and to win their liberty.

Originally, then, *ho dios Korinthos* was repeated in a reproachful and threatening manner by a spokesman for the authorities. However, it echoed back in the opposite sense; it became a cry

---

5. *The Odes of Pindar*, trans. Richmond Lattimore (Chicago: The University of Chicago Press, 1974).

6. *The Frogs*, 439.

of freedom. When children took over the cry, they did not know much about its origin, but they certainly felt the sense of it: that it echoed, mocked, and exorcised the reiterated and empty threat of the powers by which they were constrained.

Now, Socrates (if we may speak metaphorically) has been chanting *ho dios Korinthos* in the course of his exhortation. For Socrates shows how the King told the orator, who went on to tell the general, that everyone in the kingdom had to withdraw from everything real. Indeed, everyone listened. The whole Kingdom withdrew from the real. But Socrates shows, too, that the King had nothing to offer in return for this renunciation. When the world turned to gold, and eternity rose before us, we, obeying the King, most stupidly were not there.

The King had been chanting *ho dios Korinthos!*—which means fly from the happiness that comes to you. Socrates echoes him: *ho dios Korinthos!* He repeats the chant of the King in order to turn it against the King, and he longs for that which is lost.

But what more can Socrates do? He is, notoriously, an essentially negative spirit. He himself, more than anyone, has withdrawn from everything real. That is why he keeps talking, why his whole life is in talking—he wants to recapture in words the fullness which he has lost.

Everyone sees this in Socrates. The holiest of men, he is somehow detached from holiness. He therefore asks: what is holiness? The bravest of men, he is somehow detached from courage and asks: what is courage? The wisest of men, his wisdom somehow escapes him—and if he feels any wisdom within him, it is a wisdom that is altogether negative: that of knowing he does not know.

Holiness, courage, wisdom, beauty, love, justice—he lives all that. Yet he lacks the substance of his life. His life remains "out before" him, and he wants a "copy" within him. He will try to copy it in words. Of course, the enterprise is hopeless, as he knows.

A lover wants to be "one" with the beloved but remains detached however much he loves. Socrates, likewise, wants to be "one" with his life, but remains detached, however much he speaks. Love is happiness. Speech, too, is happiness, but they do not restore the substance lost.

> So then I myself, Crito, having fallen into this perplexity, began to bellow at the top of my voice, beseeching the two strangers as though calling on the Dioscuri, asking them to save us, Cleinias and me. (293a)

The Dioscuri (twin sons of Zeus) were Castor and Polydeukes. They were thought to live in the sky and were recognized in the stars. They came down, beating their wings, to aid soldiers and sailors in distress. In mysterious ways, the Dioscuri were linked to Rhea, and the attendants of Rhea were—Corybantes.[7]

So we may turn, now, to the main part of our commentary, the part on the brothers' discourse. The brothers engage ostensibly in sophistical disputations, but under the cover of these disputations, they perform certain rites—the Corybantic rites, which are rites of initiation. Their aim is to rescue Socrates, to make him "young and beautiful" again. I mean this, I think, in a rather literal way. The performance of the brothers is a rite of initiation. It follows a classical initiatory schema, with hazing, "death," acquisition of marvelous powers, ecstasy, vision, and joy. And the climax of the brothers' performance, which is a tremendous epiphany of life, resolves the problem of Socrates, which is that of remoteness from life.

Eliade writes, "initiation lies at the core of any genuine human life…In…moments of total crises, only one hope seems to offer any issue—the hope of beginning life over again."[8] Now, Socrates has reached a time of crisis, but he is going to begin life over again for the *Euthydemus* inaugurates the "middle period" of Plato—the time of Socrates's radiance.

---

7. Karl Kerényi writes: "The picture of the Tindarids (Castor and Polydeukes) is not complete unless there stands between them the shining figure of a woman, their beautiful sister or actually the great goddess, the Mother of all Gods. Rock carvings at the town of Akrai in Sicily testify to the service of the Dioscuri to the great Mother, Rhea-Cybele," *The Heros of the Greeks* (New York: Thames and Hudson: 1959), 110. Let us note, too, that Plato himself links the Tindarids with the figure of the goddess and the Curetes (= the Corybantes) in an intriguing text in the Laws (796b) in praise of ambidexterity.

8. Mircea Eliade, *Rites and Symbols of Initiation: The Mysteries of Birth and Rebirth*, trans Willard R. Taske (Putnam, Conn.: Spring Publications, 2012), 203.

Jesus said to them: "When you make two into one
...you will enter the kingdom of heaven."

                      THE GOSPEL OF THOMAS, Saying 22

I see everything twice.

                      JOSEPH HELLER, *Catch 22*

CHAPTER FIVE

*Two, not One, or
The Chairing of Cleinias*

The first thing we hear about the brothers—and I am referring, now, to the first page of the dialogue—deserves special consideration. Crito, entering the gymnasium, thought he saw Socrates talking to a stranger, but actually there were two strangers—"two, not one were present."[1]

> Who was it you were talking to yesterday, Socrates?...It seemed to be a stranger.
>
> Which of the strangers do you mean, Crito. Two, not one, were present. (271a)[2]

---

1. Concerning the fact that Crito sees only one "stranger," Hawtrey comments that "it is perhaps worth wondering why Plato has Crito make this mistake" (*Commentary*, 40). I agree, it is worth wondering—though no decisive answer can be given. "Clearly," Hawtrey comments, Plato "wished to emphasize the fact that there were two sophists" (40)—this is all that can be said with assurance.

2. The question arises as to whether the "real" Euthydemus ever performed with his brother. If, as is likely, the "real" brother of Euthydemus is the Dionysodorus who appears in the *Memorabilia* as an instructor in the art of fencing (III.1), then it must be said that this individual—who is humorously presented by Xenophon as an example of extreme mental sluggishness—probably could not have functioned as a sophist under any circumstances. I am intrigued, then, by Hermann Keulen's suggestion that Plato turned two brothers—one a fencer, the other a sophist—into a weird pair of sophists who had both taught fencing in the past (*Untersuchungen zu Platons "Euthydem,"* 12f.

This "twoness," moreover, remains obtrusive throughout the dialogue, since the strangers—the brothers—are eerily alike and have a strange way of echoing each other.[3]

Further, if we glance briefly at the parts of the brothers' performance (sharply divided by Socrates's two exhortations), we find that, in the standard pagination, the first part is three pages long; the second, six; the third, twelve. Three…six…twelve. Each part is double the last. Thus the formula "two, not one"—so conspicuously uttered by Socrates and so peculiarly embodied by the brothers—governs our text throughout.

Further, the phrase "two, not one" applies to many of Plato's writings. The bifurcation of knowledge, leading to knowledge of knowledge (*Charmides*); the bifurcation of beauty, leading to spatiotemporal beauty (*Hippias Major*); the doubling of the "One," which generates all number (*Parmenides*); the doubling of genera, which generates all specificity (*Sophist*); and (most chillingly) the slicing

---

and notes). Now, if this is so—if Keulen's view is right—it shows that Plato was determined that the adversary of Socrates in this particular dialogue should somehow present himself in the aspect of a pair. And Crito's failure to see Dionysodorus (271a) could be taken as an allusion to the historical facts of the case—that the "real" Euthydemus worked singly.

3. "The fact that the brothers are two," writes Hawtrey, "contributes…to the humor of the dialogue; Shakespeare gains a similar effect in Hamlet, by the conversion of what is essentially one character into the semi-comic pair of Rosencrantz and Guildenstern" (*Commentary*, 14). Let us note, however, that Rosencrantz and Guildenstern are exactly alike—but this is not true of the brothers. Gifford notes, for example, that Dionysodorus—"with his coarse insolence and stupid attempts at wit" is "even more shallow and ignorant than his brother," *The Euthydemus of Plato*, 11; and Hawtrey acknowledges, too (57), that Euthydemus seems the stronger of the pair. Now, we should note that Plato took an interest in patterns of this sort—that is, in patterns of duality where the two sides are almost identical, except that one is somehow "weaker" than the other. The left and right sides of the body are a striking example of this pattern, discussed in the *Laws* at length (749e); and the metaphysical significance of the left and right sides of the body is elaborated by Aristophanes in his discourse in the *Symposium*, where we are threatened with bisection along just these lines, if we persist in behaving iniquitously (190d).

of the androgens, a punishment of sin, an audacious assault on the gods (*Symposium*)—all these images and movements disclose a becoming two of one, which appears to be, as the *Epinomis* indicates, Plato's formula for very nearly everything (990a—991b), and which, in the *Euthydemus*, quite conspicuously greets us at the door.

Further, Aristotle tells us that, for Plato, the One is the ultimate good; the Two, the ultimate evil. Thus "two, not one" would mean "bad, not good" or even (roughly) "not God, but the Devil." The appearance of a figure who is two, not one, would be the least auspicious omen in the world.[4]

But Aristotle also tells us that, for Plato, the One generates form upon the Two which is equivalent to matter. Thus, "two, not one"

---

4. See Aristotle, *Metaphysics*, 988a, 1–10. As we know, the "Two" or "Dyad" figures prominently in the Pythagorean Platonism discussed by J. N. Findlay, *Plato: The Written and the Unwritten Doctrines* and by the Tübingen School commentators. See, for example, Hans Joachim Krämer, *Plato and the Foundation of Metaphysics: A Work on the Theory of the Principles and Unwritten Doctrines of Plato with a Collection of the Fundamental Documents*, trans. John R. Catan (Albany: State University of New York Press, 1990) and Giovanni Reale, *Plato and Aristotle: A History of Ancient Philosophy*, trans. John R. Catan (Albany: State University of New York Press, 1990). To situate my work with respect to these commentators, I offer the following remarks. (1) It seem to me a fact that we can discern within Plato a Pythagorean system based on the One and the Dyad. Findlay's work shows this clearly, and Krämer and Reale (only recently published in English) also make a powerful case. (2) On the other hand, I suspect that Plato was sufficiently "Socratic" to remain somewhat skeptical about the system he was developing. That is why the system remains latent in his dialogues, and why the pieces of the system—as we see in the great work of Cherniss, who, however, exaggerates the difficulties—do not always neatly fit together. (3) Finally, if we wish to understand the One and the Dyad in Plato, we must not only think like philosophers and mathematicians but also like literary critics. For the One and the Dyad are not mere abstract principles. They are the basis of worlds of immensely concrete experience. And they are frequently elaborated in the literary aspect of Plato—in images, stories, and so on. (Krämer, let us note, proposes an alliance between "literary" interpreters of Plato, such as Sinaiko, Rosen, and Burger, and the commentators of the School of Tübingen [*Plato and the Foundation of Metaphysics*, 38]).

would mean, "not form, matter"—that is, "dissolution of form," "reduction to the latencies of matter." Socrates, it seems, requires such an experience in order to obtain the abundance of life he seeks. "Let them decimate me! Let them do with me what they want to! Let them boil me down if they must!" (285c).

However, our task is simply to study the chairing of Cleinias, the first part of the brothers' exhibition. The chairing works on several levels at once, and these we consider separately—advancing from philosophy and sophistry to mysticism, ritual, and myth. But the phrase, "two, not one," rules on each of these planes. It is the theme of the rest of this chapter, and in a way, the rest of this book.

1. *The Two Questions*

> Who are the learners? (275d)
>
> What do the learners learn? (276d)

These are the questions that the brothers put to Cleinias in the course of the ritual chairing. The questions prove to be exactly alike, except that the first (who learns?) concerns the subject of the learning process, whereas the second (what do we learn?) concerns the object.

The relation of subject and object is a special problem for Socrates. All that maneuvering of Socrates in his exhortation to Cleinias, all that talk about the "future" and "utility," all those nervous departures from a world that grew ever more abundant (and at the same time ever more threatening,) all that floating in a basket (to speak with the poet Aristophanes)—all this may be said to illustrate the space between subject and object to which the brothers, with their questions, allude as they go to work.

The brothers are "two, not one"; likewise the subject and object. "Two, not one" means "bad, not good." The subject-object split is our misfortune. But just as, in the *Parmenides*, the repeated division of the One gradually restores us to a state like the undivided One, so, too, here. The brothers—who are "two"—restore the One when they finish their work.⁵

2. Contradictions

> Euthydemus began, as far as I can remember, in terms very much like these. Cleinias, he said, who are the learners—the wise or the foolish? (275d)

> Seeking to astonish us still further...Euthydemus went on with his questioning...Now, do the learners learn what they know, he asked, or what they don't know? (276d)

Here we have the "complete" version of the questions that the brothers put to Cleinias, and our impression of "twoness" grows stronger. To each of two questions, there are two possible answers; and Cleinias—the answerer—is forced to choose between them.

The first question is: who are the learners—the wise or the foolish?

—When Cleinias replies that the wise are the learners, Euthydemus points out that the wise have no need to learn because they already know.

—When Cleinias replies that the foolish are the learners, Dionysodorus points out that the foolish cannot learn because they lack the capacity.

The second question is: what do the learners learn—what they know or what they do not know?

—When Cleinias replies that the learners learn what they do not know, Euthydemus points out that what is altogether unknown is unintelligible, therefore unlearnable.

---

5. The plan of curing duality with duality reminds us of the plan of curing motion with motion, discussed by Plato in the *Laws*. Nurses, Plato says, quiet their babies by rocking them, thus curing motion with motion; and the secret rites of the Corybantes, as Plato adds explicitly, work in exactly this way (790c). Now, the identification of the Corybantes with nurses points to Chora, the "Nurse of Becoming" or Plato's principle of matter (*Timaeus*, 47e), and this confirms the suggestion that the performance of the brothers is connected to the principle of matter (i.e., The Dyad or *mega-kai-smikron*).

—When Cleinias replies that the learners learn what they know, Dionysodorus points out that to learn is to acquire knowledge, and we can only acquire what we do not already possess.

Who, then, are the learners, and what do the learners learn? The answer to the question is that those who are wise and foolish learn what they know and do not know.[6]

But of course, this is only a game; the game of contradiction. The sophists of antiquity liked to play this game, and we even have a text—the anonymous *dissoi logoi*—which shows how the sophists played it, how profound they made it, and how silly. Plato, too, liked the game. When Plato explains in the *Republic* that beautiful things are also ugly and just acts also unjust, and that, quite generally, all things have opposite qualities (479a–d), he is saying, in effect, that life in the world has been arranged in such a manner, that the game of contradiction can and must be played at all times.

According to Plato, life's contradictions have a teleological aim, and this, too, is described in the *Republic*, in a text of the greatest significance. The text appears in Book Seven, directly after the cave. Its point—somewhat simplified—is this: Self-consistent things—hands that are merely hands, trees that are merely trees—are of little inspiration to us; for they simply are what they are, and do not stir the mind to thought (523c). But inconsistent things, duplicitous things—the large that is small, the dark that is bright—these things stir the mind because they are two and one at once (524b), and they perplex us, rouse us from rest, and make us dream of a truer, richer world. These things, accordingly, deserve to be called

---

6. According to Sprague (*Plato's Use of Fallacy*, 5–6), the argument about learning combines two distinct fallacies, that of equivocation (since the Greek work *manthano* means "to learn" and "to understand") and that of taking absolutely what should be taken only accidentally (since "knowing one's letters" becomes "knowing without restriction" and this, in turn, becomes "wise"). In a remarkable way, Sprague succeeds in showing that virtually all the brothers' arguments are based upon these two fallacies—that their whole world, with its eerie terror and beauty and its vulgar, raucous humor—is erected on the basis of these two simple sleights of hand.

"The Summoners" or "The Exhorters" (523c). Apart from "The Summoners," we would remain in a sleeping state.

It seems, then, that as we watch the brothers play contradiction with Cleinias, we discern in them the aspect of "The Summoners," of life in its aspect as summons. Sitting on opposite sides of Cleinias and speaking in opposite ways, they represent the ambiguity that rouses our fallen humanity—the salvific "twoness" of things.

3. *The Echo Effect*

Let us note, too, that the structure of the chairing is designed to heighten the "twoness" under discussion. The "script" below (composed mainly of citations) shows in what sense this is so.

FIRST QUESTION

> Euthydemus (*to Cleinias*): Who are learners, the wise or the foolish?
>
> Dionysodorus (*grinning in Socrates's ear*): I am pleased to announce in advance that whatever the boy says will be found by us to be mistaken.
>
> Cleinias: The wise learn...
>
> Euthydemus: The foolish!
>
> Cleinias: The foolish...
>
> Dionysodorus: The wise!

SECOND QUESTION

> Euthydemus (*to Cleinias*): Do learners learn what they know or do not know?
>
> Dionysodorus (*grinning in Socrates's ear*): Here comes another one, just like the first! All our questions are like that: once in, you can't get out of them.
>
> Cleinias: Learners learn what they don't know...
>
> Euthydemus: What they do know!
>
> Cleinias: What they do know...
>
> Dionysodorus: What they don't!

Everything echoes, everything happens twice: the question, the conspiratorial whisper, the pattern of refutation—A-B-B-A. What, then, is really going on?

Here we begin to approach the peculiar depth of the performance. The "echo effect" is a mystical effect—it belongs to the onset of Dionysian ecstasy. Proof that this is the case may be obtained from *The Bacchae* of Euripides, the last of the great Attic tragedies. Let us turn, then, to *The Bacchae*.

The play speaks of the conflict between the cold, aggressive, stereotypically "masculine" Pentheus, and the ecstatic, androgynous, preternaturally "quiet" Dionysus. However, the difficulty is that Pentheus is only a man, whereas Dionysus is a "god-man," rising to the fullness of divinity. Obviously, Pentheus is doomed.

Now, a moment comes, in the last third of the play, when the god-man Dionysus, in the guise of a beautiful youth, succeeds in "tempting" Pentheus, whose resistance has so far been obstinate. Tempted, Pentheus sees. In the place of the beautiful youth, he sees a beast, a bull. At that moment the doubling begins.

> Pentheus: I see two suns blazing in the heavens.
> And now two Thebes, two cities, and each
> With seven gates. And you—you are a bull
> Who walks before me there...
> Have you always been a beast?
> But now I see a bull.
>
> Dionysus: It is the god you see.[7]

The best interpretation of this text is the most literal. The onset of Bacchic experience—the moment when the god Dionysus overturned the normal sensibility—must have been characterized, at least for many initiates, by a certain perceptual distortion: the whole world seemed to alter, everything doubled, echoed, happened twice. The last line of our text, "It is the god you see," is certainly meant to be ambiguous, but perhaps it is meant to suggest that the god Dionysus is everything Pentheus sees: the beast, the youth, and the doubling movement itself.[8]

---

7. Euripides, *The Bacchae*, 918.
8. We have one other classical drama about Dionysus—Aristophanes's

Here, too, I think, we approach the deepest level of the dialogue *Euthydemus*—the secret of the brothers' performance. There were many cults in Athens that sought Dionysian experience—among them, that of the Corybantes.

4. *The Rites of the Corybantes*

> Do not be surprised, my dear Cleinias, if the arguments of our visitors seem queer to you, for perhaps you do not see what they are doing to you. They are acting like the celebrants of the Corybantic rites when they perform the chairing of the person they are going to initiate. There, as you know, if you have been through it, they have dancing and playing; and so these two are dancing and playing around you, as they prepare for your initiation. (277d)

What do we know about the Corybantic chairing? We know, of course, that it was the preliminary part of an ordeal of initiation. The novice sat in a chair (his "throne") and the celebrants danced around him, "raising a great din."⁹ The word

---

The Frogs; and here again, let us recall, the theme of "twoness" figures prominently. For Dionysus appears with a double (the servant Xanthias and the confusion of their identity (which occurs over and over) provides many opportunities for laughter. At the end of the drama, moreover, Aeschylus makes an appearance, and he establishes himself as the greatest of all tragedians by reciting a line that runs as follows: "Chariot upon chariot, corpse upon corpse was hurled." The line, to be sure, seems unmemorable, but we can see that Dionysus likes it, and as he gives the palm to Aeschylus, he explains his delight in these words: "Two chariots and two corpses he put into the scale: Why, a thousand Egyptians couldn't lift it!" (1405) It is as if the god's secret—as well as the secret of tragedy—were contained on a vast field of death, where "twoness" was everywhere present.

9. James Hillman points out in *Suicide and the Soul* (Thompson, Conn.: Spring Publications, 2020) that the Greek word *thronos* is related, through the root *dher* (carry, support), to *therapeia* (care), as well as to the Sanskrit *dharma* ("'habit' or 'custom' as 'carrier'"). "Here," Hillman writes, "we strike an etymological root of the analytical relationship. The chair of the therapist is indeed a mighty throne constellating dependence and numinous projections. But the analysand also has his chair" (93). The chair suggests stability; but the therapy itself has its "wild and whirling" aspect. There is a *Dionysian*

peribombouminos ("raising a great din") appears in several descriptions of the rite.[10]

We know that the dancers were armed; swords clashed around the novice. We know that the music played in the rite at times had peculiar effects: the heart beat quickly, the breath came quickly, hallucinations ensued, and so on.[11]

We know, finally, that the chairing was unpleasant for the person undergoing it. Sitting quietly on his chair, feeling, doubtless, somewhat vulnerable and self-conscious, the novice was disoriented by the "din" going on around him—going on, somehow, for his sake.[12]

Now we can see how this applies to our text.[13] The brothers, obviously, "raise a din" around Cleinias, and do so, it seems, for his sake

---

element in it, which counterbalances the distance that is also obviously necessary. Hillman writes, "With the help of Dionysus an analyst is better able to get caught by the drama of the patient, to enter madness and be torn apart, to let the woman in him show, to admit his animal shape and be impelled by the brute drives of power, of raw laughter, of sexual passion, and the thirst for more and more. Dionysus offers involvement in suffering" (99).

10. For example, Celsus in Origen, *Contra Celsum*, 3 and Lucan in *Lexiphranes*, 9. Cited by Ivan M. Linforth in "The Corybantic Rites in Plato," *The University of California Publications in Classical Philology* 13, no. 5 (1946).

11. See, for example, Longinus, *On the Sublime*, 39.2. Let us note, in this connection, that sound is of the greatest importance in Corybantic mysticism: in order to see, one must first of all hear. Crito, we recall, explains rather pointedly that he had trouble hearing the performance of the brothers, and though he did manage to see well enough, he strangely "missed" Dionysodorus (271a).

12. Lucian, for example, writes: "We have had enough drinking and reading...I, at any rate, am quite drunk and sick to my stomach, and if I do not promptly get rid of all these disquisitions of yours, I shall find myself in a Corybantic state, I believe, amidst the din or words with which you have deluged me." Linforth, "The Corybantic Rites in Plato."

13. Chance writes: "Socrates likens the entire experience [of Cleinias] to the performance that attends the chairing of the initiate into Corybantic mysteries. Like those who minister unto such rites, Socrates explains, the brothers are just dancing about, raising a din of intoxicating music, and causing him to lose consciousness of everything but the whirling rhythms of their logic, all to induce him to submit, in Corybantic fashion, to forces outside himself." After this excellent description, Chance unfortunately adds: "There is a sig-

(275d). They are like dancers (276d); their pupils, like a chorus (276c). The argument floats back and forth (277b); the "chorus" shouts on cue (276c); the rhythm of the performance at last becomes insupportable. Cleinias blushes, looks about helplessly (275d), and seems increasingly dazed. He is said to be "going under" (*baptizomenon*) when Socrates calls for a rest (277d).

But perhaps what remains most striking about the performance is the use the brothers make of their "twoness," their "duality." We learn at 271b that the seating arrangement is like this: Euthydemus/Cleinias/Socrates/Dionysodorus, which means that Cleinias is assaulted by men on opposite sides of him—men who elaborate arguments which point in opposite ways. Now, it happens that there is a story (preserved by Clement of Alexandria) in which a Corybant is murdered by two of his brothers;[14] and, in a variant of the story, the name of the victim is Kelmis (probably "Knife") and his killers are Akmon and Damnameneus, whose names mean "Anvil" and "Compeller" (or Hammer). Now the pertinence here is obvious; for Cleinias—the knife—is crushed between the brothers as between an anvil and hammer. He is being made virtuous: he is therefore destroyed and transformed.[15]

Further, many myths and sagas use similar images of obstacles coming together to suggest, precisely, the resistance one must encounter in passing to a higher world or state:

---

nificant respect in which the brothers are inferior to the Corybantic ministers...They are powerless to deliver the final rites, which are intended to cap the ceremony by returning the neophyte to a state of calm and tranquility. In Plato's vivid portrayal, then, the brothers are suddenly transformed into the phony ministers of pseudo-philosophical mysteries, and as such, they are the perfect foil for Socrates, who...[can] accomplish the initiation in the true sense" (*Plato's Euthydemus*, 48–49). But why is Chance in such a hurry to describe the brothers as "phony?" Clowns they certainly are, but they are not phony clowns. They are real clowns as anyone can see. Why also cannot they be real mystics?

14. Clement of Alexandria, *Protrepticus*, 2.19.

15. The following sources are cited by Karl Kerényi in *The Gods of the Greeks* (London/New York: Thames and Hudson, 1951), 85: *Scholium to Appolonius of Rhodes*, 1.1126; Ovid, *Metamorphoses*, 4.281; Sophocles, fr. 337.

> The *vagina dentata*...the Symplegades...the "clashing rocks," the "dancing reeds," the gates in the shape of jaws, the "two razor-edged restless mountain," the "two clashing icebergs," the "active door," the "revolving barrier," the "door made of the two halves of the eagles's beak," and many more—all these are images used in myths and sagas to suggest the insurmountable difficulties of passage to the otherworld.[16]

Add to this the Hydra and the Crab, which threaten to crush the hero Hercules, and to which, in our dialogue, the brothers are explicitly compared (296c). But this passage through crushing obstacles—to what, precisely does it lead? What is the higher state gained?

5. Rhea and the Corybantes

It seems that, all across the Aegean, a Goddess, a Great Mother, "the Mother of Gods and Men," was envisioned with a train of male attendants, usually dancing, armed youths. The Great Mother had many names: Rhea, Cybele, Adrasteia, etc. Her attendants, too, had many names: Ceuretes, Caberoi, Dactyloi, Telechines, and, most frequently—Corybantes. The Corybantes, then, may be viewed as "primal beings"—of all beings, the closest to their source.

Of Rhea, it is said that she is "the mother of gods and men," the source of heaven and earth; that all riches, all abundance, all happiness flow from her;[17] that she loves the castanets of the worshipers who are devoted to her; that she loves—"...the clamor of wolves/And the cries of bright-eyed lions,"[18] that she is a liberator and savior—but in a certain way "a deceptive savior;" that she is "The Mountain Mother" and "rejoices in frenzied fighting;" and that she "delights in mankind's horrid screams."[19]

---

16. Mircea Eliade, *Rites and Symbols of Initiation: The Mysteries of Birth and Rebirth*, trans Willard R. Taske (Putnam, Conn." Spring Publications, 2012), 110.

17. "Orphic Hymn XXVI."

18. Homeric Hymn "To the Mother of God," trans. Charles Boer in *The Homeric Hymns* (Columbus, Ohio: The Swallow Press, 1970).

19. "Orphic Hymn XIII."

Of the Corybantes, it is said that they are the greatest initiators—the first of all initiators;[20] that they are gigantic, handsome youths; that they are deformed, wizened dwarfs;[21] that they are the first miners and smelters—in effect, the founders of the iron-age;[22] that the frenzy they arouse in their worshipers ends in a kind of tranquility and is therefore a "purifying" frenzy;[23] that they cause and cure madness;[24] and that they are the howling wind.[25]

The rites of the Corybantes originated in Phrygia. From there they were widely disseminated. The aim of these rites was possession, *enthusiasmos*. The celebrants, we read (in Eustathius's citation of Arrian) "are possessed by the Corybantes and become Corybantic...They rush about, shout, dance, foretell the future... They yield to madness in honor of Rhea."[26]

Let us stress what Arrian says. The celebrants, he says, are "possessed by the Corybantes" and "yield to madness in honor of Rhea. The celebrants, in other words, first "become" Corybantes, and then, as Corybantes, achieve a vision of Rhea; a vision of the source of all that lives.

Returning to our dialogue, we may expect the performance of the brothers to end with just such a vision. So we return to the problem left unsolved in our chapters on Socrates. Socrates "floats" above life and cannot find his way back to life. But the brothers have come to help him. Life itself will come forth at their hands.

---

20. The Corybantes were identified with the Curetes, the initiators of Zeus.
21. See Kerényi, *The Gods of the Greeks*.
22. See the discussion in Mircea Eliade, *The Forge and the Crucible: The Origins and Structures of Alchemy*, trans. Stephen Corrin (New York: Harper Torchbooks, 1962).
23. Plato, *Laws*, 790d.
24. At the opening of *The Wasps* of Aristophanes, two slaves are conversing. One, responding to something strange done by the other, asks, "Are you really off your head or are you possessed by the Corybantes?" (8). As for curing madness, see *Laws*, 790d.
25. "Orphic Hymn XXXVII."
26. Eustathius, *On Dionysus Periegeta*, 809

What they did,
they did for Dionysos,
for ecstasy's sake:
Now take the basket,
think;
think of the moment you count
most foul in your life;
conjure it,
supplicate,
pray to it;
your face is bleak, you retract,
you dare not remember it…
What they did,
they did for Dionysos,
for ecstasy's sake;
Now take the basket—

                                  H.D., "At Eleusis"

CHAPTER SIX

The Harrowing Transition

Having heard the first part of the brothers' presentation, Socrates complains that they are merely playing games and asks that they become "serious." So when, after a break, the brothers resume their performance, it is natural that Dionysodorus should turn the tables on Socrates and ask whether "seriousness" is really what everyone wants:

> Tell me Socrates—and all you others too—when you say that you desire this youth to be made wise, are you merely playing games, or is your desire true and serious? (283*b*)

Socrates replies, for the crowd, that their desire is true and serious.

We can easily imagine that, in the actual Corybantic rites the ministers did what the brothers are doing here. At a certain point they paused and inquired whether the friends of the novice were "serious" and wished the completion of the rite. The company assured them that they were all "serious"—but the atmosphere suddenly chilled.

> Some people [writes the physician Aretaeus] slash their limbs, with the pious notion that they are doing something pleasing to their gods, who, they believe, expect this of them. Their madness is limited to this assumption on their part, because they are sane in all other respects. They are roused by pipes and gladness of heart or drunkenness, under the instigation of other people who are present. This madness is called enthusiasm. If they endure to the end, they are happy and free of distress, believing that they have experienced the sacrament of god; but they are pale and emaciated, and

the weakness caused by the pain of their wounds lasts for a long time.¹

The references to pipes, infection, enthusiasm, show that the cult being described is of the Corybantic type. The cult offered joy, but the joy included pain. The cult was extremely "serious."

But the terrible event expressed by the brothers discourse is not (or not yet) the ecstatic self-inflicted torment described by Aretaeus; it is, on the contrary, something sober, severe, constrained. The victim is going to be Cleinias. Cleinias, in fact, is going to be ritually sacrificed; and certainly this would be serious if it were not merely a joke—merely a joke about murdering the boy.

> Tell me, Socrates, said Dionysodorus, you want this youth to become wise, don't you?
>
> Certainly, I said.
>
> Well, is he wise now or not?
>
> He says he's not; he's not a braggart...
>
> So what he's not, you want him to be. And what he is, you want him to stop being. You want him dead! Why what excellent friends and lovers you are! You desire your darling dead at any price! (283*d*)

In this "cartoon" of the rites of the Corybantes, where the ancient cult of ecstasy merges with "modern" sophistry, the sacrifice of Cleinias appears as the main event. The rite which is being caricatured is a rite of initiation, and the price of initiation is—death.²

---

1. Aretaeus, 3.6.11. Cited in Linforth, "Corybantic Rites in Plato," 147.
2. Concerning the joke about murdering Cleinias, Sprague comments as follows: "The argument appears trivial enough but is actually of considerable significance, since it is based on a metaphysics incompatible with Plato's, namely, that of Parmenides. The essence of Parmenides' philosophy was, of course, that what is is, and what is not is not; consequently, there is no becoming (*Plato's Use of Fallacy*, 13)." It seems, then, that, with the joke about murdering Cleinias, the brothers, for the first time, show their philosophic colors: they are Eliatics, successors of Parmenides. Now, Eliatic philosophy is plainly rooted in mysticism—it is rooted, in fact, in Parmenides own chariot-experience, which leads, let us recall, through "the gates of night and day," to

Nor is this surprising. In virtually all rites of passage, all over the world, the death of the novice is represented symbolically for the novice is "dying" to his old way of life. (Plato, too, understood that this had to be so, and, in the *Phaedo*, he speaks of it unforgettably for he says that philosophy, the supreme initiation, is nothing else than "a practice of death.") We may say, then, that the old—the merely human—Cleinias "dies" in the brothers' performance, and a new, radiant Cleinias—the Corybantic Cleinias—is born.[3]

It is to be expected that from the time the brothers tell their joke about murdering Cleinias, Cleinias seems dead. He says not another word during the rest of the brothers' performance. In the third part, he laughs for a moment, and his presence excites Ctesippus (300*d*). We may see this is to symbolize the moment of his rebirth.

But who "killed" Cleinias? Certainly not the brothers, who represent the Corybantes, but rather Socrates and Ctesippus, who "desire their darling dead." The scenario is that the brothers, having "chaired" and danced around Cleinias, hand him over to others who "kill" him. But who might these others represent?

Perhaps they represent Titans. There is in fact a well-known myth, to which Plato alludes in the *Laws* (701), in which the Curetes (= the Corybantes) dance around the infant Dionysus, whom they have seated on the ground, or perhaps in a chair or on a throne. One vaguely imagines the scene—the wild, mystical dancers, the tiny vulnerable child, the impression that the dancers are going to hurt the child. But suddenly, certain other figures appear; terrible figures, whose faces are whitened with chalk. These figures are the Titans (*titanos* means chalk). They take the child and kill him. They

---

the great goddess's epiphany (fr. 1). Now, the brothers also seek such an epiphany—by a peculiarly dark and especially clownish route.

3. Another view of the joke, which takes account of its "seriousness," is that of Monique Canto. She says that the point about the joke is that the desire to make people wise is, in the end, incompatible with loving them, since it means, precisely, rejecting them as they are. This dilemma, Canto notes, is a constant problem for Socrates, who is thereby "reduced to silence," while Ctesippus aggressively steps forward (*L'Intrigue philosophique*, 138).

dismember, boil, and roast him, and eat him in a sacrificial meal. The Titans, in short, receive the child whose death they desire from the dancing Curetes or Corybantes. Just this scenario unfolds in the *Euthydemus*, where the brothers are the dancers, the divine child isᲪleinias, and Socrates and Ctesippus—cast in the role of Titans—desire Cleinias's death.[4]

Our task, of course, is not to reconstruct the myths and rites of the Corybantes, but to understand Plato's text, and if possible, his mind. Cleinias is to be "sacrificed" (so, at least, runs the joke), but he is assured of being resurrected (this happens at 300d). Meanwhile, his death bears many fruits. How so?

Let us recall, in this connection, the two exhortations of Socrates. Socrates speaks of a perfect world, a superabundant world, a world of gold, of immortality—a world he lacks. He lacks it because he flees from it. It is there. He can sense it. It beckons at every moment, but at every moment, he flees from it. In his basket, he floats away. That is why he "bellows" for the brothers.

Now, the brothers agree to help, but their condition is the sacrifice of Cleinias. First, they conduct Cleinias through a certain mysterious "twoness." Then, they speak of his death. Everyone, they say, desires the death of Cleinias—and we will see that the death of Cleinias, to the degree that all acquiesce to it, will restore the superabundance that for Socrates has slipped away.

Let us begin at the beginning. From the point of view of Ctesippus, Dionysodorus has told a desperately sick joke for Ctesippus, as we know, is particularly fond of Cleinias. It does not amuse him at all to "desire his darling dead." But it is always hard to know how to deal with a "sick" joke. If one does not attack the joke, then repulsive, sinister words hang unchallenged forever in the air. If, on the

---

4. There are many versions of the myth, but I have given the one recounted by Clement of Alexandria (150?–220? CE), which fits our dialogue perfectly. Clement writes: "The mysteries of Dionysus are utterly inhuman, for when he was still a child and the Curetes were dancing their dance in arms around him, the Titans came secretly upon him, and lured him with childish toys, and tore him limb from limb," Abel, *Orphica*, 196.

other hand, one does attack the joke, one appears as a bad sport who cannot distinguish playfulness from seriousness.

Ctesippus, however, is a fine, manly youth, and he attacks the joke with alacrity.

> Ctesippus, on hearing this, was agitated on behalf of his favorite, and said: Stranger of Thurii, were it not a rather discourteous thing to say, I would say to you frankly to be damned, sir, for speaking so falsely of me and my friends as to suggest a thing too unholy to be even uttered—that I could desire the destruction of this boy. (283e)

Ctesippus speaks in the fierce but measured tone of a gentleman demanding satisfaction. He has taken the joke seriously. His honor demanded that he should. He has turned straight to Dionysodorus and has said, "You lie!" Now he pays the price of his seriousness.[5]

1. *The Lie*

> What! said Euthydemus. Do you think it's possible to lie?
>
> To be sure, I do, Ctesippus replied. Unless of course I'm raving like a maenad.[6]
>
> In that case, tell me this: When you lie, do you do it by speaking of the thing of which you speak, or by not speaking of it?

---

5. At this point it becomes clear that the brothers are going to offer, not merely word-play and argument, but also a plot, a scenario: Socrates and Ctesippus are cast in a weird drama (about friendship, death, truth, etc.) which they know to be merely a fantastic contrivance, but which at times they feel to be real—so real they almost take it "seriously." Dionysian consciousness obviously lends itself to theater, to full participation in imaginary scenarios, and sometimes, too, it finds "real life" merely theatrical, as when Plato describes us as "toys" or "puppets" of the gods (*Laws*, 1). James Hillman writes: "Dionysian consciousness is the mode of making sense of our lives and worlds through awareness of mimesis, recognizing that our entire case history is an enactment…and that to be 'psychological' means to see myself in the masks of this particular fiction that is my fate to enact," *Healing Fiction* (Thompson, Conn.: Spring Publications, 2019), 46.

6. Hawtrey notes (*Commentary*, 99) that the colloquialism *ei me mainomai* appears in Aristophanes's *The Clouds* (660). I've provided a literal translation ("unless I'm raving like a Maenad") instead of the usual "unless I'm crazy."

By speaking of it, he said.

Then, if you speak of it, you speak of nothing else, in the whole realm of being, except that of which you speak?

True.

And this thing you speak of, it's a single thing, isn't it, distinct from all the others that are?

Yes.

Then if you speak of it, you speak of what is?

Yes.

But anyone who speaks of what is and things that are is of course telling the truth. So Dionysodorus, since he speaks of things that are, tells the truth concerning you, and is not lying. (283e)

If you take a joke seriously, you may find that, far from getting rid of it, you get entangled in it. This is what happens to Ctesippus. Euthydemus tells Ctesippus that he, Ctesippus, definitely wants Cleinias dead. He necessarily wants Cleinias dead because Dionysodorus has said so, and what Dionysodorus says cannot fail to be true, since lies are impossible, and all statement are true.

Most people dream occasionally of grotesque situations from which they cannot escape, since the means of escape—which would normally be easy and obvious—have been bizarrely and inextricably closed. Such is the case with Ctesippus. He is accused of something unspeakable, and the obvious escape is to give his accuser the lie. But the escape is cut off if there is no such thing as lying.

Is there not a further complexity here? Is there not a strange ambivalence? Can we not help feeling drawn to a world without lies? Can we not help actually desiring it? It seems, in fact, that the dream of murdering Cleinias is linked to a dream of joy, for if lies were really impossible, if all human utterance were true, if truth were so close to us that no one could ever depart from it, or even desire to depart from it—would we not find Paradise again?

As for the argument proposed by Euthydemus, it works best in Greek, where various phrases in it equivocate bewilderingly,[7] but it does not depend on equivocation, and its drift, I think, is this. Even if I lie—assuming I really can lie—I speak of the thing of which I speak. I "speak of nothing else, in the whole realm of being, except that of which [I] speak" (284a). So if I say, for example, that the sky is blue, I am talking about a blue sky—not about a grey sky. If you, at the moment, are acquainted with a grey sky, that is all very well but that is obviously not the sky I mean. In the same way, Dionysodorus speaks of a Ctesippus who wishes to murder Cleinias, and his words can only refer to a Ctesippus with this wish. There may be another Ctesippus, or another side to Ctesippus. There may be, indeed, a gentle, honorable Ctesippus—but that is not the Ctesippus of whom the brothers are speaking, although this gentle, honorable Ctesippus might be the theme of another speech. Ctesippus, then, is guilty as charged, and Cleinias will be (or has been) sacrificed, since in the new world of truth that the brothers' discourse opens up for us, all the friends of Cleinias desire Cleinias's death.

Of course, there is only one way for Ctesippus to reply to this. All he can reply is that there is no such thing as a Ctesippus who wants to murder Cleinias—and that it is possible, accordingly, to formulate a statement that does not refer to anything that is. "If you speak like Dionysodorus, you are not speaking what is (284b)."

But all readers of Plato know what the brothers are going to say next. If you do not speak what is, you speak what is not. In an

---

7. For Sprague, the equivocation in the joke about "speaking of things as they are" depends on the verb "to be" (here *ta onta*) which, Sprague says, "is taken in two senses, as meaning either "to exist" or "to be true" (*Plato's Use of Fallacy*, 13). Another equivocation is suggested by Gifford (*The Euthydemus of Plato*, 36)—an equivocation on the verb *legein* that can mean "to speak a thing" (e.g., a word or sentence) or (more properly) to speak *about* a thing" (the object of the discourse). Virtually all commentators agree that the Eliatic being, which excludes all becoming, all distinction, etc.—is in some way meant to emerge in this argument; but I want to connect this emergence to the joke about murdering Cleinias, which is, after all, its cause.

inconceivable manner, you bring nothingness into your discourse. It seems, then, that the innocence of Ctesippus hangs by the thread of non-being, which is certainly the slenderest of threads.

2. *Non-Being Is Not*

> The things that are not, Euthydemus asked, surely are not?
>
> They are not, Ctesippus replied.
>
> And nowhere, presumably, is where the things that are not are...
>
> Yes...
>
> Then is it possible for anyone to deal with these things—that is, the things that are nowhere—so as to make them in some manner be?
>
> I do not think so.
>
> Now, tell me this: Think of rhetoricians speaking before the crowd—do they do nothing or something?
>
> They do something.
>
> And if they do something, they make something?
>
> Yes.
>
> Speaking is doing and making?
>
> Yes.
>
> So, then, it is clear that no one speaks what is not—for thereby he would be making something; and certainly you have agreed that no one can make what is not—so that, by your account, no one speaks what is false; while if Dionysodorus speaks, he speaks what is true and is. (284*b*)

The argument depends on taking strictly the apparently valid assertion, "The things that are not are not," and its more picturesque equivalent, "The things that are not are nowhere." If the Ctesippus who is a murderer does not exist, then, of course, he is nowhere. The difficulty, however, is that discourse is a "somewhere." If the murderer Ctesippus exists in a discourse, then he also exists in reality for you cannot make a discourse, which obviously exists, out of something that does not exist at all.

The drift of the argument is to show—what is in fact perfectly true—that the lie presupposes the actuality of the negative. In order to tell a lie, I must cause "that which is not" to enter into my discourse and extract my discourse from truth; and "that which is not," if it really and truly is not—if it lacks, as Plato has said, that faint trace of being that preserves its very non-being—can, of course, do no such thing (see *Parmenides*, 162b).

Therefore, we may conclude, "if Dionysodorus speaks, he speaks what is true and is" (284c). So the sacrifice of Cleinias has perhaps already taken place, for Cleinias is quiet like the dead. What, then, is happening here?

Two phrases float to the surface and haunt this part of the dialogue—"the things that are not are not," and "you desire your darling dead." This is what the phrases, when taken together, mean: we desire the conquest of nothingness; we desire that being flourish; we desire a world in which non-being is not and death itself is dead. But then we must desire our darling dead for the price of this fullness is precisely a death or a sacrifice—in this case, the sacrifice of Cleinias.

Ctesippus, of course, still resists what the brothers keep repeating. Ctesippus declares that he does not wish Cleinias dead and needs to retain non-being, so as to give the lie to the brothers. To be sure, it is only a joke, but Ctesippus takes the joke seriously—as if a joke could cause the death of Cleinias. In fact, the seriousness of Ctesippus in the face of a joke illustrates the point the brothers are making which is that being clings to our words, and language has magical power.

But what Ctesippus argues now is this. If anyone says of Ctesippus that he desires the death of Cleinias, then, let us admit, that person is speaking of what is. He is saying what is to the degree that there are actual entities (the actual Ctesippus and Cleinias) who provide a content for the discourse. "But somehow, speaking of what is, he does not speak it as it is (284c)." The accuser speaks of what is but not as it is, because Ctesippus would never murder Cleinias. Ctesippus is Cleinias's friend. But can we really speak what is only not as it is?

3. *Speaking of Things as They Are*

How do you mean, Ctesippus? asked Dionysodorus. Are there really people who speak of things as they are?

Why, certainly, there are gentlemen; and gentlemen always speak truth.

Come, then, and answer me this: Good things are in good case, but bad in bad, are they not?

Yes.

And you admit that gentlemen speak of things as they are…

I do.

Then, Ctesippus, the good speak badly of the bad, if they speak of them as they are.

Yes, they do; I am sure they do. I am absolutely sure that the good speak badly of the bad—and you yourself, sir, if you care to listen to me, will beware of being included among the bad, lest the good speak badly of you. For they speak badly of the bad, I assure you.

And they speak greatly of the great, and hotly of the hot?

Certainly, I presume, sir. For they speak frigidly of the frigid and call their way of arguing frigid.

Help ho! Abuse! Abuse! (284*d*)

Of course, this is not an argument in the sense of a "philosophical" argument. It is a dark and comical absurdity, which the brothers are happy to have caused.

Thanks to this absurdity, we descend deeper into the realm toward which the brothers are leading. If Socrates and Cleinias do not resist what is happening, they will soon discover that they are—"speaking of things as they are." They will speak hotly of the hot, lengthily of the long, badly of the bad, dully of the dull. They will soon reach a point where the distinction between words and things becomes so subtle and attenuated, that things, rather than words, will appear to arise from their mouths.

If non-being is not, Plato suggests in the *Sophist*, then being and its name amount to the same thing; for being cannot not be its name (244d). That is the whole truth of it. We are descending in that direction here. Soon, being will merge with its name. We shall traverse the language of dreams, where meanings present themselves as images, and pass round the language of sorcerers and witches, of which Socrates speaks at 390a in our text. We will arrive, then, at the "true" and "primal" language, the language of being that bodies forth what it names; the language of sheer creativity.

But all of this only angers Ctesippus, who is trying to demonstrate his innocence of murder and who has not been allowed to proceed. Vast and implacable powers are causing the friends and lovers of Cleinias to desire the death of Cleinias. The more Ctesippus struggles, and the more he resists this desire, the more surely he descends into a realm of richness and strangeness—a realm for which, quite possibly, he has always secretly yearned, and for which this death is the price.

Now, philosophy, for Plato, is itself "a practice of death"—but one always assumes this refers to one's own death. Here, however, it means the other person's death. Ctesippus rises to being; Cleinias undergoes death.

Happily, none of this is serious, but Ctesippus, of course, persists in taking it seriously. He could laugh, shrug his shoulders. He could scorn the ridiculous performance and simply walk away from the game. Instead it seems that he wants to win the game, so he is taking it more and more seriously.

When Ctesippus, in his frustration, insults and threatens Dionysodorus, and Dionysodorus yells, "Help ho! Abuse!" Socrates finally intervenes.

4. *The Cauldron and the Cave*

> Ctesippus, my feeling is that we should receive from our guests what they say, if they are willing to give us this gift, and not quarrel over a word. If they know how to do away with people so as to change them from wicked and foolish to wise and good...then let them, by all means, destroy the lad for us and make him wise, and let them do it to the rest of us, too. (285a)

This is the first conspicuous discussion in Plato of the link between wisdom and death. The second conspicuous discussion appears in the *Phaedo*. There, we read that, in order to gain wisdom (i.e., view the realm of forms), we must practice death (i.e., "die" to the world as a whole). In spite of the many objections raised against the *Phaedo*, it remains one of the most exhilarating texts in the history of Western thought.

It is odd, on the other hand, that a "nightmare" version of obtaining wisdom through death should precede the sublime rendition of it.[8] But Plato had a freakish sense of humor, as A. E. Taylor has said.[9]

Let us note, too, that though Socrates is willing to consent to the death of Cleinias, he is even more willing to consent to his own death. For the "death" proposed by the brothers, though it contains a promise of resurrection, still seems hazardous. Yet Socrates feels that, since he is an old man, he should take this risk.

> I am an old man and I am not afraid to take risks, and I put myself into the hands of Dionysodorus as if he were Medea of Colchis. Let him decimate me, let him do with me what he wants to, let him boil me down if he must. Only he must make me good (285*c*).

I have already spoken of this text; but here, I have two further comments. First, the magic cauldron of Medea belongs to a whole series of such vessels, including that of Pelops, to which our text quite definitely alludes at 304*b*, and that of Dionysus—boiled in a cauldron by the Titans but reborn as Semele's son—to whom our text alludes in several places.[10]

---

8. As a matter of fact, the earliest portrait of Socrates "practicing death" happens to be a comic one, though slightly creepy. As Hawtrey and others note (*Commentary*, 105), 285*c* of the *Euthydemus* seems to be based on a passage from *The Clouds*, in which the elderly pupil Strepsiades, who wants to learn how to "think," is placed by Socrates on a mattress filled with bedbugs—as if, in order to think, one must submit to being devoured (see Hawtrey, *Commentary*, 105). Plato is always wrestling with Arisophanes's portrait of Socrates in *The Clouds*, trying to sort out the true and the false in it. Socrates himself, who was forty-five when he saw the play, may have been hit hard by it. The intellectual crisis he describes in the *Phaedo* (96*a*–97*c*) might well have been caused by it.

9. Taylor, *Plato: The Man and His Work*, 45.

10. See the discussion in Kerényi, *The Heros of the Greeks*, 273.

Second, the speech about the magic cauldron marks a change in the attitude of Socrates. He had formerly been distant and ironic, and had mostly "just listened" to the brothers. Now, on the contrary, he is active in the performance, increasingly absorbed in the rite. For Socrates is an old man. He needs the help of the brothers. He needs to be immersed in Medea's magic cauldron, to be made "young and beautiful" again.

"And I too," Ctesippus says,

> will surrender myself to the strangers, and they can skin me, if they like, even more than they are doing now. I ask, however, that my hide not end by being made into a wine skin, which is what happened to the hide of Marsyas, but that it be made into the shape of virtue. (285c)

The torture spoken of by Ctesippus, that of being flayed (having to shed one's skin) has, of course, an initiatory significance. There is, for example, a Tantric meditation in which "the novice imagines that he is being stripped of his flesh and sees himself, finally, as a huge, white, shining skeleton." Then, too, we find "this same initiatory theme in Siberian and Eskimo Shamanism."[11]

Now that Ctesippus has decided to put up with "skinning," he naturally desires to be reconciled with his tormentors. So he speaks the following words:

> Dionysodorus believes that I'm vexed with him; but that's not true; I'm not vexed with him at all; I merely contradicted certain remarks which I seem to remember him saying of me, which I thought were improperly said. Come, now, my generous Dionysodorus, do not call contradiction abuse: abuse is quite another thing. (285d)

Assured in this way that he has not been abused, but only contradicted, Dionysodorus replies that this is impossible, since there is no such thing as contradiction (285e). The argument of Dionysodorus "echoes" that of Euthydemus at 284, and we need not consider it further.[12] The "skinning" process continues until 286b, where Socrates once again speaks.

---

11. Eliade, *Rites and Symbols of Initiation*, 166.
12. Discussing this and subsequent arguments, Chance assumes that the

5. *The Tragic Vision*

Ctesippus now fell silent, but I, marvelling at the argument, said: Look here, Dionysodorus, the substance of your statement is that there is no such thing as speaking falsely—is that not so?

He agreed.

Then would you say that, while no one can speak falsely, one can, at least, think falsely?

Not that either, he said.

So there is no false opinion, I said, at all?

No, he said...

Nor ignorance, nor ignorant men—for ignorance, if it were possible, would occur when we put things falsely.

Certainly.

But there is no such thing as this, I said.

No, he said.

Well, Dionysodorus, what I am going to say may strike you as somewhat pedestrian, but you will have to forgive me. Here it is: if no one ever speaks falsely, or thinks falsely, or is stupid in any way, then, I suppose, no one ever makes mistakes in doing anything, either. For, in doing it, there is no mistaking

---

brothers could not possibly be serious and are indulging "merely in philosophical sport." Perversely aided by "lack of commitment to the truth" and by "much-needed distance from subject matter," they can "concentrate on mechanics"—on "overall grace" of performance (*Plato's Euthydemus*, 101). Chance shows well how the brothers mirror certain frivolous distortions in philosophy including that of our own time (e.g., wild game-playing or absurd narrowness). But it is a question of deciding in what way, and to what extent, the brothers lack seriousness. Chance agrees that the core of their arguments comes partly from Parmenides, and Parmenides, a mystic—enlightened by a goddess—was certainly a serious man. Now, why should not this ancient seriousness still linger in the brothers, along with a clownish pleasure in "philosophical sport?" As for truth, if by that we mean something like "ultimate" truth, there is not much hope of stating it directly, as Plato concedes in his famous Second Epistle. Why not try to hint at it, then, by drawing one's hearers into a bizarre and elaborate scenario, a tragi-comedy that keeps getting wilder?

the thing done. You will put it like that, will you not?

I shall. (286c–287b)

The magic language—the language without lies we have considered in this chapter—thus brings forth, at Socrates's own hands, a marvelous new world, a world of inerrant human beings. Let us consider what this means.

The sense we have, at virtually every moment of our lives, that we are doing, saying, or thinking less than we ought, or something other than we ought, that we are falling short of an ideal somehow assigned us, an ideal whose force we acknowledge, and that other persons, too, are falling short of an ideal—all this must disappear in the world opened up by the brothers. For here, nothing falls short. Here, all obtain the ideal. Here, thoughts, words, and deeds always turn out perfectly, for here, as Socrates puts it, there is no *hamartia*, no "error": "For, in doing it, there is no mistaking the thing done."

We know, however, that this marvelous world feeds on blood. Sacrifice sustains it. Hideous demands are connected with it. "Flay me!" "Boil me!" "Let them do with me what they want to!" "Desire your darling dead!"

So we arrive at a question. Why should perfection come from terror? It is perhaps not possible to answer this question directly, but we should note, at least, that the question is a familiar one, for it recurs, in a way, in every Greek tragedy we have.

Agamemnon, Clytemnestra, Orestes, Electra, Deianira, Hercules, Jocasta, Oedipus, Creon, Medea, Phaedra, Agave, etc. etc.—every single one of them, either knowingly or unknowingly, "desires a darling dead" and is "boiled" and "flayed" in turn. How does this carnage strike us? Somehow, it strikes us as beautiful. It has about it a transcendental rightness as if the gods themselves had desired and contrived it. And we may go so far as to whisper to one another that it is all so perfect, so luminous, so rich, that none of the agents portrayed in it can have made any sort of error—as Socrates would put it, "For, in doing it, there is no mistaking the thing done."[13] But let us go further.

---

13. Commentators have not been much interested in discussing the question of tragedy in connection with these pages (286c–287b), but there are good

The word *tragodia* means "Song of the Goat"—the song of the goat to be sacrificed. Tragedy develops from the festival of Dionysus, and it appears to reenact, in a special "poetic" form, what was once a sacrificial rite. Now, what is the reason for the rite? What is the purpose of blood sacrifice?

I would like to present three comments concerning this question—comments that shed light on our text. The first is from Eliade, the second from Sjöö and Mor, the third from George Bataille.

Eliade writes:

> All evidence indicates that blood sacrifice, and human ones particularly, were performed by agricultural communities. Never by hunters...It's quite an odd thing, when you think about it...For primitive man, the animal is there, it is given...[But] man creates a harvest...[And] by performing a blood sacrifice, one is projecting the energy—the "life"—of the victim into the work one wishes to create.[14]

Sjöö and Mor write:

> Individual sacrifices, often voluntary...occurred only among settled agricultural people. Why? Because settled

---

reasons for doing so. The reasons are: (1) Plato is interested in tragedy. (2) The joke that sparks the discussion concerns the murder of a youth by his friends; and tragedy arises, as Aristotle tells us, when "the killing is done between friends" (*Poetics*, 14). (3) The word *hamartanien* ("to miss the mark, to err, to go wrong") obtrudes at this point in the dialogue (287b), a word that appears in Aristotle's treatise on tragedy (in his discussion of the tragic "flaw") and was probably used before Aristotle in earlier discussions of tragedy. (4) The word *spoudaios*, which appears in our dialogue whenever Socrates demands seriousness of the brothers (287c, 288c, 300e), also figures prominently in Aristotle's treatise on tragedy, as when Aristotle says that the tragic hero is *spoudaios* (good, weighty, serious, etc.) in contrast to the *phaulos* (or "low-down") hero of comedy; here, once again, it is likely that Aristotle is using a "standard" critical vocabulary. (5) The plan of "curing motion with motion," ascribed by Plato to the Corybantes (see Chapter Five, note 5) reminds us of the plan of purifying "pity and fear" by arousing them. This is described by Aristotle (in a somewhat elliptical manner, as if he were referring to a view familiar to his hearers) as the "final cause" of tragedy.

14. Mircea Eliade, *Ordeal by Labyrinth: Conversations with Claude-Henri Rocquet*, trans. Derek Coltman (Chicago: The University of Chicago Press, 1982), 58.

agricultural people, during the Neolithic, were taking control of the growing processes of earth. They were deliberating planting, deliberately reaping. And they felt this intentional use of the [earth's] body might be a violation; it needed propitiation...rebalancing...reharmonizing.[15]

Bataille writes:

> Sacrifice destroys an object's real ties of subordination; it draws the victim out of the world of utility and restores it to that of unintelligible caprice. The sacrificer declares: I belong to the sovereign world, the world of gods and myths, of violent, uncalculated generosity...I withdraw you, victim, from the world in which you were...a thing. I call you back to the intimacy.[16]

There you have the essence of it. With the discovery of agriculture, the world was sown, plowed, used in various ways, but it was no longer given. It was no longer fully present. It withdrew into the distance—Paradise was lost. Then came the moment of sacrifice. Someone was boiled, someone was flayed, someone desired his darling dead, and as the horror built to a climax, another world was born; the sacred world of our dreams. That happened many, many times. It happens for us still in any tragedy, where the deed of horror calls forth a radiant perfection—the "wholeness" mentioned by Aristotle. And it is happening to Socrates, too.

Socrates, in the course of his two exhortations, speaks of a distant, empty, merely "useful" world and an anxious, aimless humanity. Then, he "bellows" for help (293a). The brothers, coming to help, offer what Socrates longs for—a richer, stranger world, a world that is fuller in its being—but plainly the price is steep.

"I have lost the beauty of the world," cries Socrates. "I only know how to use it, and its uses are weary, stale, and flat. I am floating away, in a basket." "We can help you," say the brothers, "but you must die and inflict death. We will flay you, boil you, and do with

---

15. Monica Sjöö and Barbara Mor, *The Great Cosmic Mother: Rediscovering the Religion of the Earth* (San Francisco: Harper & Row, 1987), 178.
16. Georges Bataille, *Theory of Religion*, trans. Robert Hurley (New York: Zone Books, 1989), 44.

you what we want to; and you shall first put Cleinias to death." But how did Plato feel about these horrors?

In fact, we know how he felt. As a youth, we are told, he wanted to write tragedy—which means he was drawn, for a time, to what the brothers offer, this mixture of holiness and dread. However, Plato changed. Though tragedy never ceased to move him, he became more aware of the unwholesome element in it. At last, in the *Republic*, he broke with it entirely, explaining himself in this way: God, he declares, is good, and is responsible only for good (379*b*), and has nothing in common with the eerie dreamworld of wizards (*goetes*), where beings alter ceaselessly and evil forms haunt the night (380*d*; 381). Therefore there is no numinous evil, no recapture of holiness through evil.[17] Since tragedy seems to teach us that the gods themselves are manifest in evil, tragedy ought to be banned (380*a*).[18]

We will speak again of tragedy later. Here we return to our text. The brothers, we recall, have declared all humans infallible (287*a*) and the particular case of the infallible human Socrates is discussed and settled in what follows.

6. *Reversal*

> You are uttering rubbish Socrates, and you are not answering our questions...
>
> Yes, I said, I seem to have gone wrong; certainly I am quite stupid. But perhaps, after all, I did not go wrong. Do you think I went wrong Dionysodorus? If I'm right, you know, you won't refute me, no matter how clever you are; but if I'm wrong, why then, its really you who are wrong, for you say we're incapable of error...But my view of the matter, Euthydemus and Dionysodorus, is that the argument remains where it was: it's playing a game of "knock-down-tumbledown," just as it always has. And all your art—with

---

17. Paul Ricoeur's theory of tragedy is based upon Plato's critique. See his *Symbolism of Evil*, trans. Emerson Buchanan (Boston: Beacon Press, 1969), esp. 211–27.

18. On "Plato's Anti-Tragic Theater," see Nussbaum, *The Fragility of Goodness*, 122–36.

all its wonderful accuracy—has yet to redeem it from this failure. (288*b*)

The second part of the brothers' performance is drawing to a close. It now occurs to Socrates (as it has perhaps occurred to the reader) that the arguments of the brothers are self-destructive.

This is the reason. The brothers are defending the assertion that error is impossible: "For, in doing it, there is no mistaking the thing done" (287*a*). But what can the brothers say to Socrates, when he denies their assertion, insisting that error is possible. If they think that Socrates is right, then, of course, they will not refute him, no matter how clever they are for they are seekers after truth. But if they think Socrates is wrong, then, of course, it is really they who are wrong for they are asserting that no one is capable of error.

Now, all children, East and West, past and present, play a game we refer to as "Knock-Down-Tumble-Down" (*katabalon piptein*) or "Loser Wins." The idea of the game is that one child tries to trip another, and if he succeeds, he immediately falls down himself, as if his opponent's defeat had toppled him. Now, the brothers arguments are like that. They collapse if their opponent is beaten. They suffer, Socrates says, "from *katabalon piptein*"—despite their "accurate reasoning" (288*b*).

In fact, a certain giddiness now appears to come over Socrates, as he finds that any phrase he utters—whether brilliant or idiotic—will instantly decimate his adversaries. The brothers, as Socrates comments, are assuredly "awesome in fight" (271*d*). But awesome in fight though they are, their extinction can be procured by the slightest word set against them, by the slightest, least audible breath.

All things considered, then, Socrates really is infallible in his fight against the brothers. Yet this means losers win, so the brothers win.

7. Fade-Out

Here is a final observation. The question of winning and losing matters little for the conversation is starting to fade out as if it had never taken place. Someone speaks. We listen. We think something is happening, yet when the words have been spoken, they do not slip into the past but into a sphere of dreams.

At 286e, for example, we listen to a conversation that may be summarized like this:

> Dionysodorus: There's no such thing as refutation.
>
> Socrates: Yes, there is.
>
> Dionysodorus: Then refute me!
>
> Socrates: Why do you ask me to refute you when there's no such thing as refutation?
>
> Dionysodorus: I didn't.

The end of the exchange is an "awakening," which reveals the beginning as a "dream." In the end, we arrive at an argument that seems—but perhaps only seems—to remove from the conversation the last traces of reality. The argument runs like this:

> You must tell me, Dionysodorus, I said, what your phrase can possibly intend.
>
> Well, just answer me this, Socrates, he said... Is there life in things that have intentions, or do lifeless things have them too?
>
> Only those things that have life, I said.
>
> Now do you know any phrase that has life?
>
> By heaven, sir, I don't.
>
> Then why did you ask me what my phrase intended? (287d)

The argument, in Greek, puns on the word *noein* ("to think" and "to mean") and points out that, since only living things *noein* ("think"), then words and phrases, which are not alive, cannot *noein* ("mean") anything at all. The argument leaves us with a dilemma according to which either life and soul are everywhere, or speech is mere sound without sense. In the second case, the whole conversation flows back into a kind of clamor. We understood nothing about it, because there was nothing to understand—it was nothing at bottom but a "din."

In the first case, on the contrary, we are placed in a new world where life animates everything and all things swell with soul and life. This is the world of ecstasy.

All these things—the chestnut tree, the bandstand, the statue by Velleda in the laurel thicket—abandoned themselves to existing like those tired women who relax into laughter murmuring in a tired voice: "it is good to laugh." I saw that there was no half way between non-existence and this swooning overabundance. If you exist at all, you have to exist to this point: to the point of swelling, of moldering, of obscenity.

JEAN-PAUL SARTRE, *Nausea*

The overflowing richness of reality...which haunted all great poets...is for Sartre a looseness, an obscenity (the word is inevitable).

GABRIEL MARCEL, *Existence and Human Freedom*

CHAPTER SEVEN

The Final Revelation

We turn, now, to the brothers' third exhibition, which expresses the condition of ecstasy or *mania*. Here, at last, is the final revelation. It is a revelation of the measureless aspect of reality—of being in its overabundant richness.

Knowledge (293*b*), power (294*b*), shame and degradation (294*d*), a small bit of gold (299*d*), an unidentified drug (299*b*), a man's hands and arms (299*c*), the whole flesh of a man (299*b*), one's mother (298*d*), one's father (298*c*), etc. etc.—all these (and more), as soon as the brothers speak of them, swallow up the boundaries which had formerly held them in check, and rise to face us, swelling ceaselessly. Let us consider this enlightenment more closely.

In the everyday world—the world of ordinary consciousness—beings, plainly, are structured and constrained. This chair is only a chair—it remains within the limits of a chair. This tree is only a tree—it remains within the limits of a tree. And we ourselves, in the same way, remain within certain limits. The sphere of our presence, our wisdom, strength, and power, the length of our days, our suffering and iniquity—all are allotted to us within certain definite limits, and these limits make us what we are.

But the aim of the brothers has been to lift this veil of limits. At the start of their performance, they induce an impression of doubling, which is a first step toward the limitless; then, in the transitional part of the performance, they deny the reality of the power of the negative, which is in fact the only power by which being might have been constrained. And now we come to the last part of the performance, which is the full exploration of the limitlessness of being. The brothers are going to show that no part of being can in any way be constrained; for the tiniest trace of being—if it *is* in any way at all—expands and expands beyond measure.

> Masses we find to be limitless... And if we take what seems to be a minimum, suddenly, as might happen in a dream, what we took to be one appears many, and what seemed to be least appears large (*Parmenides*, 164d)

This swelling, self-rending substance has for Plato many different names. He calls it the Dyad (the Two, *he duas*) to stress the aspect of self-rending; and he calls it the Great-and-Small, since the smallest part of it is great.[1] But Plato also speaks of it as the Nurse of Becoming (*Timaeus*, 49b), and thus sets in relief the "maternal" aspect of it. As the deep substance of things, it is the source from which all arises; and its mythical precursor is the Great Mother herself—Adrasteia, Rhea, or Cybele.[2]

Here, then, at last, we arrive at what is serious in the brothers' exhibition.[3] The brothers, as Socrates says, are ministers of the

---

1. As reported by Aristotle, *Metaphysics*, 988a14.

2. On the connection between the Great Mother and and the principle of expansiveness (which is also that of embodiment), James Hillman writes: "For the mothering attitude, it is always a matter of life and death; we are obsessed with how things will turn out; we ask what happened and what will happen. The mother makes things 'great,' exaggerates, enthuses, infuses the power of life and death into each detail because the mother's relation to the child is personal, not personal as related and particular, but *archetypally personal* in the sense that the child's fate is delivered through the personal matrix of her fate, becoming fate in general which she then is called. The mother archetype gives the personalist illusion to fate. Whatever she has to do with takes on overwhelming personal importance which actually is general and altogether impersonal," "Abandoning the Child," in James Hillman, *Loose Ends: Primary Papers in Archetypal Psychology* (New York and Zurich: Spring Publications, 1975), 36. Reprinted in *Uniform Edition of the Writings of James Hillman*, vol. 6: *Mythic Figures*.

3. When I say that the brothers will now become "serious," I am not forgetting that, given their particular character, their most serious moment will also be their giddiest. But I do mean to oppose the view expressed by

Corybantes (277d) and they yield, in Arrian's phrase, "to madness in honor of Rhea." And everything we discussed in the last two chapters of this book—the magic language of truth, the queer sense of inerrancy, the hazing, the doubling, the boiling, the flaying—all these things, although perhaps at times more than play (*paidia*), are still less than serious (*spoudaios*): they merely provide a transition—at times, to be sure, a harrowing transition—to the "madness in honor of Rhea" that Socrates now wants to see.

> Our visitors [Socrates complains] have not really been serious in the displaying of their wisdom...instead they are merely bewitching us (*goeteuonte*)...But let's grab them and not let them go until they reveal to us what is truly their serious object. If they ever start to be serious, something entirely beautiful in them will, I feel, shine forth. (288b)

Let us note, too, that the "entirely beautiful" experience that Socrates seeks from the brothers is the solution to the difficulty he described in his two exhortations—and this, precisely, is the overarching difficulty of Socrates's whole life. For Socrates, let us recall, has detached himself from being and longs to be immersed again in being; and the brothers stand precisely for intimacy with being—being swells and flows forth at their hands.

However, there is a difficulty.

The difficulty is that the experience offered by the brothers cannot be embraced without grave reservations, because it continues to exhibit that perverse and eerie violence which so often distressed us in the last chapter of our commentary. Thus the brothers offer everything—but not in the right manner. Or the brothers offer the

---

Hawtrey, which is a fairly representative one. "The longest scene of the dialogue," writes Hawtrey, "rises to a climax...of hilarious nonsense, containing a total of thirteen sophisms. There is little community of theme among these...On the whole they are too trivial to be taken very seriously, except for their undoubted value as logical exercises" (*Commentary*, 140). Now it seems to me—and I will try to show in this chapter—that the content of the brothers' discourse in this part of the dialogue is in actual fact quite rich, and the "community of theme" quite marked. Hawtrey, too, finds valuable fragments in the discourse (see notes 9, 14, 20, etc.)—but insists that the whole comes to little.

goddess (Cybele, Rhea, etc.)—but it is not the right goddess; or perhaps it is the right goddess, but viewed in the wrong way.

At the end of this book, we speak briefly of this difficulty, taking as our guide the verse that Socrates quotes to the brothers—Pindar's "Water is best." Our present task, however, is to turn to 293*a*, which is where we left off in our reading of the dialogue. Socrates, let us recall, is wandering in a maze (291*b*) and chanting nonsense like a child (292*e*), for he has failed to discover the particular art he is seeking, the art that—

> Sits by itself
> At the helm of the city,
> Steering the whole,
> Commanding the whole,
> Conferring a use on all beings. (291*d*)

The brothers, however, appear to be acquainted with an art that answers this description, and when Socrates "bellows" for help (293*a*), they immediately rush to his aid. Let us see what sort of aid they give.

1. *Boundless Knowledge*

> Do you desire, said Euthydemus, that I instruct you in the knowledge that has baffled you so long, or shall I convince you that you have it.
>
> Convince me that I have it, for heaven's sake, I said. That will be much easier than learning for a man at my time of life.
>
> Come, then, and answer me this: do you know anything?
>
> Yes, many things. However, they are trifles.
>
> Ah, but that will suffice! Now tell me whether it seems possible to you that anything at all—anything in the world—should in truth not actually be the very thing which it is.
>
> That, I replied, seems impossible.
>
> Now you, he said, know something?
>
> Yes.
>
> Then you are knowing, if you really know.

Yes, of course, I replied, in just that something. But there are many things I do not know.

Then if there is something you do not know, you are not knowing.

Not knowing, at least, in just that thing, I replied.

Are you therefore any less not knowing? But just now, Socrates, you said that you were knowing; and so, here you are, exactly the man you are, and then again not that man—and with respect to the same matter, and at exactly the same time, too.

So be it, Euthydemus, I said, and it's certainly "good news to me," as they say. But I would like you to tell me how I gained the knowledge we were seeking. The reason seems to be that it is in fact not possible for the same thing to be and not to be—so if I know one thing, it's evident I know all—for I could not both know and not know. But then, since I know everything, I have the knowledge I seek to boot—for isn't that your point Euthydemus? Isn't that your wisdom?

Yes, you see, Socrates, your own words refute you. (293*b–e*)

Socrates wishes to learn the all-encompassing art by which being as such is made "useful," and the brothers assure him that he already knows what he asks. He already knows what he asks because in fact he knows all things. In fact, he is omniscient—like a god. But in what sense is Socrates omniscient?

Socrates, let us admit, knows at least a little—he knows a few unillustrious truths. But if Socrates is knowing, he cannot be not knowing. So if Socrates can grasp the tiniest trace of truth, he knows, at least implicitly, the realm of truth as a whole. *Eiper hen epistasai, panta epistasai*—if you know one thing you know all (294*a*).[4]

---

4. Chance writes: "In their latest manifestation, our two sorcerers stand before us as the answer to...the Socratic search for the supreme science... They themselves solve the enigma by becoming its solution...For just a brief moment then Plato allows us to imagine the two-headed philosopher-comedian at the helm, piloting the ship of state and rendering all things good and useful. And yet behind this distorted image, in part grotesque, in

Now the day is fast approaching—in the dream world of Platonism—when a passionate, mystical Socrates will repeat this lesson in the *Phaedrus*. He will speak of knowing oneself (230*b*) and of discerning the god in oneself (250*b*). He will show that to be human—to discern in the flux of sensation the outline of stable truth—is to know, in advance, with an obscure but potent knowledge, the realm of truth as a whole (249*c*). So *eiper hen epistasai, panta epistasai*—and what the brothers teach Socrates, Socrates teaches to Phaedrus. For to know the nature of even the dreariest, most mediocre object is to grasp, precisely, the oneness of this object; and this entails an implicit knowledge of what it means to be "one," which is perhaps the most inclusive of all truths (249*c*). But where did we acquire this potent *a priori* knowledge? We won it before our birth, on the other side of the sky (247C). And how can we awaken this now buried knowledge? It is *mania* that awakens it—the lover's, poet's, prophet's, mystic's madness (244–45).

All this we read in the *Phaedrus*. But the day in which Socrates speaks in this way has not arrived in the dialogue *Euthydemus*; the *Euthydemus* merely prepares for it. For we encounter in the *Euthydemus* the "old homely" Socrates of Plato's early dialogues, not the "young beautiful" Socrates of the middle-period works. The old homely Socrates is the skeptical Socrates—the man who keeps insisting that "he knows that he does not know." And when lovers, poets, and other evokers of *mania* approach skeptical Socrates with a plan to release the boundless knowledge within him, the

---

part amusing, we can also see that everything the brothers appear to be is contradicted by what they are..." (*Plato's Euthydemus*, 138). But what do the brothers appear to be? Surely "philosopher-clowns," as Chance calls them, and this is exactly what they are. Their comedy, moreover, masks their seriousness, as is usually the case with great comedians. Chance admits, for example, along with many other commentators, that the brothers' argument here—knowledge of one equals knowledge of all—is thoroughly Platonic, so, as Chance says, "the latest piece of eristic buffoonery is meaningful," after all. Chance feels sure, however, that the brothers are unaware of the meaning: it is "different from what [they] intend (138)." Yet, one would think that anyone clever enough to construct these weird, obtuse arguments would be clever enough to clearly grasp the point of them.

resistance they encounter is naturally fierce; fierce but perhaps not invincible.

For when the brothers speak of boundless knowledge, Socrates seems to be interested—and his bright, sardonic manner does not conceal this interest. Socrates asks many questions concerning boundless knowledge, thus inviting the brothers to explain its nature in detail. The first question appears below.[5]

2. *Boundless Power*

> In the name of goodness, Dionysodorus, I said, I can see that now at last the two of you are serious; before I could hardly prevail on you to be so. But really, do you two know everything? For example, carpentry and shoemaking?
>
> Certainly, he said.
>
> And are you proficient at leather-stitching?
>
> Why yes, in faith, and also cobbling.
>
> And the stars, Dionysodorus, do you know how many there are? And have you numbered the grains of sand?
>
> Certainly, he said…
>
> Now, for my part, Crito, I here became quite incredulous, and at last felt compelled to ask if Dionysodorus also knew how to dance.
>
> To which he replied: Certainly.
>
> But I don't suppose, I said, that you have gone so far in wisdom as to be able to do a sword dance and be whirled about on a wheel—not at your time of life?
>
> There is nothing, he replied, that I cannot do. (294*b*)

If one really knows all things, then, of course, one knows how to do all things. The brothers assure Socrates that they can do all things. No task for them is too great, no task for them is too dull.

---

5. The comic aspect of the discussion of absolute knowledge is nicely captured by Canto, who speaks of it as presenting a "caricature of sophia." (*L'Intrique philosophique*, 170–75).

So Socrates asks about a few ridiculous things—about carpentry and cobbling and counting the stars and the grains of sand. The brothers say they can do these things; they declare this without hesitation. But why is it that, when Socrates interrogates the brothers about the powers to which they lay claim, the image of a sword dance fixes itself in his mind, and he feels "compelled" to ask them if "at (their) time of life" they are capable of doing a sword dance?

The reason, we may suppose, is that the powers the brother are claiming have been achieved in Corybantic ecstasy, and Corybantic ecstasy expresses itself in dancing; particularly in a sword dance of an arduous sort.

Why is it that Socrates speaks of the brothers' old age? Is it not that he is also old and anxious about age? But ecstatic possession was known to make people feel young again,[6] and Socrates longs for new vitality (285c).

Nor is dancing the only expression of the power evoked by the ecstasy. We read of the Bacchae—closely linked by Plato to the Corybantes—that they raced up mountains, wrestled wild beasts, drew milk and wine from stones, caused heavy objects to levitate, miraculously deflected spears that were thrust into them, and caused flowers to blossom with preternatural speed.[7]

What, then, can the brothers do? There is nothing they cannot do (294e). Yet, Socrates must think it over carefully before giving himself over to the experience offered by the brothers; for the brothers are unleashing knowledge and power without limit. There is a dark side to the limitless, as Ctesippus now points out.

---

6. Hawtrey cites Euripides's *The Bacchae* (184)—where the aged Cadmus and Teiresias wander off to the mountains to dance in the rites of Dionysus, assured, as they say, of miraculous rejuvenation (*Commentary*, 147). A similar reference to the miracle of rejuvenation is found in Aristophanes's *The Frogs*, 345.

7. For the miracle of the "one-day vines" (*ephemeroi ampeloi*) see Euripides, fr. 226, and Sophocles 234. The other miracles mentioned are described in *The Bacchae* (see, for example, 667–773). Plato speaks of these things in the *Ion*, 534a.

3. Boundless Degradation

> Here Ctesippus broke in: In God's name Dionysodorus, I wish you'd offer some proof of what you are saying, so I might know you were telling the truth.
>
> What kind of proof would you like? he asked.
>
> I would like you to tell us, he said, how many teeth Euthydemus has. And he, how many you have.
>
> But isn't it enough to be told that we know everything?
>
> No, naturally not; but tell us this one thing, and prove the truth of your claim. Let each of you declare how many teeth the other has, and let us, by our counting, prove you to have known it, and we will trust you, I promise, in all else.
>
> Well, they thought we were teasing them and weren't willing to do it, but they confessed they knew all things, one after the other, in response to the questions of Ctesippus. And of course there was nothing—not even the most shameful things—that Ctesippus didn't ask them before he had done with them; but they valiantly encountered each of the questions he put to them…like boars when driven up before the spears. (294c–d)

The boundless knowledge and power with which the brothers are tampering is not the "pure" sort, which grasps and manipulates sublime essences only, but the darker, stranger sort, which ranges impartially over "dirt, mud, and hair," to cite the examples in Plato's *Parmenides* (130d).

For the brothers lay claim to a knowledge and a power that are boundless in every direction and in every possible way. They are therefore well acquainted with the most luminous secrets of heaven, but they are also well acquainted with the basest secrets of earth. They know the number of hairs on our head and the number of teeth in our mouth. They possess boundless life, but they also know how it feels to suffer, and they know how it feels to die. If we think of the most wicked acts, or the most painful, grotesque, and degrading acts, we may be sure that the brothers know how to perform them, and know how it feels to want to perform them. For there is nothing they cannot do and nothing they do not know; no act, thought, or passion is too base for them.

Everyone has heard of the horrors that flow from Dionysian ecstasy—the self-inflicted wounds, the rending of the flesh, the sexual license, the extremes of degradation. Now, these terrible things express a state of mind in which everything is possible because all limits have vanished. The brothers, in their way, express this too.

As the brothers make their extraordinary confession—a god's confession about life as lived beyond limits—they seem to turn into beasts before Socrates's troubled gaze: "like boars…before the spears…they…encountered each of the questions" (294*d*). Now, the boar is a Dionysian animal as much so as the bull in whose form the god appears to Pentheus. The divine boars that are envisioned by Socrates are cruelly tormented by spears that are thrust into them, for it belongs to them to suffer this pain.[8] But the question we want to answer is whether Socrates will refuse the sort of knowledge the brothers are offering, or whether, on the contrary, he will stand firm and endure it. We will answer that question below.

4. Boundless Time and the Moment of Decision

> Now, said Euthydemus, answer me once more: Do you know what you know by means of something, or not?
>
> I do, I replied: by means of my soul.
>
> There it comes, he said; you are answering more than you were asked. I did not ask you to identify the means of your knowledge, but to tell me, simply, if in fact you know by some means.
>
> You are right, Euthydemus; you are right. I answered more than necessary through lack of education. But you will have to forgive me, and I shall now state simply that I know what I know by some means.

---

8. See Aristophanes, *The Frogs*, 348. Also see the curious notes about boars and bulls in Joseph Campbell, *The Masks of God: Primitive Mythology* (New York: Penguin, 1987), 70, *passim*.

And do you always know by this means, he went on, or sometimes by this and sometimes another?

Always, I replied, whenever I know, it is by this means.

Really, Socrates, he said, you must stop adding these qualifying phrases.

But I am so afraid the word "always" will bring us to grief...

Not us, my dear sir, but if anyone, you. But come, now, and answer: Do you always know by this means?

Always, I said, since I must withdraw the "whenever."

Then in truth you always know by this means! But do you—always knowing—know some things by this means, and others by another; or everything by this means?

I know everything by this means, I replied; everything, that is, that I know.

There it comes again, Socrates; those same qualifying phrases!

Well, I withdraw my "that is, that I know." (296a–c)

We can see where Euthydemus is intending to guide Socrates. Through an ambiguous use of the words "always" and "everything," Socrates is to declare that he always knows everything. He is to confess, in other words, that he possesses the boundless knowledge that the brothers wish to show in him and that, further, he has always possessed this knowledge; has possessed it from before the dawn of time. However, Socrates resists what the brothers are saying and refuses to make the confession which is demanded of him. Easily grasping the strategy of his interlocutors, he tries to subvert it by adding qualifying words to his replies.

Does he always know by the means by which he knows? Certainly he does—that is, "whenever I know." Does he know everything by the means by which he knows? Certainly he does—that is, "everything that I know." Now the words "always" and "everything," carry boundless knowledge to Socrates, but Socrates wards them off and so gains a reprieve.

But here is a curious fact. The brothers grow angry at Socrates when he tries to "parry their thrusts" by making use of qualifying phrases. They speak to him sharply, as if such parrying were forbidden. Everything happens as if a set of rules existed—rules to which Socrates had promised to conform, against which his phrases contravened.

> Really, Socrates you must stop adding these qualifying phrases. (296*b*)

> There it comes again, those same qualifying phrases (296*c*).

Now, if qualifying phrases are forbidden to Socrates, he will be entirely defenseless against the brothers' assaults. How, then, does Socrates reply? Should he not claim the right to defend himself? Socrates, in fact, will not claim the right to defend himself, because he does not really desire to resist the brothers' instruction. He has made up his mind to submit.

This decision to submit occurs at 295*d*, in a text we have not yet cited. Here, the brothers approach Socrates with their deathless knowledge, and Socrates tries to resist them, pretending not to understand what he is told. He keeps repeating the word "soul"—as if it could somehow protect him. Euthydemus suddenly protests: "You won't answer our questions, and you will drivel on inanely because, my dear sir, you are a tedious old fool" (295*d*). "Here," comments Socrates, "I perceived that he was annoyed. And being minded to take lessons from this new teacher, I decided I'd better give in" (295*d*).

Such is the submission of Socrates. Socrates, to be sure, does not give in altogether, and he does not give in all at once His submission is masked with his rich and much admired irony. But submit, in a way, he does, for when he is told to withdraw the qualifying phrases that ward off the knowledge borne by the "always" and "everything," he protests only a little and then quickly does as he is told.[9] So, the

---

9. Sprague comments that Euthydemus, insisting on the retraction of the words "always" and "everything," proceeds "more or less over Socrates's dead body" (*Plato's Use of Fallacy*, 24).

brothers triumph. The absurd device of sophistical disputation is set aside temporarily, and Euthydemus speaks as he desires.

> You have admitted, now, Socrates, that you always know, and know everything. So it's clear that even as a child you knew, both when you were being born and when you were conceived; and before you came into being and before heaven and earth existed, you knew all things, since you always know. Yes, and I declare, he said, that you will always know all things, if it be my pleasure. (296d)[10]

In short, there is here no debate. The dark and terrible knowledge will emerge in the mind of Socrates, if it be Euthydemus's pleasure. Socrates cries out, "O let it be your pleasure, most worshipful Euthydemus,[11] if what you say is really true" (296d). Still we have yet to discover the depth of knowledge that the brothers offer to Socrates. There is a final step to be taken, as Socrates now forsees.

---

10. Here I cite Hawtrey: "In this paragraph, Euthydemus reaches a peak of triumph, which he celebrates with an almost hymnic recitation of ages. The victory will however seem a hollow one to the reader, who has watched Socrates's handling of the argument...At the same time there is no doubt that in his hymn of triumph Euthydemus is made to refer, all unwittingly, to the anamnesis theory of learning" (*Commentary*, 155; see also Friedländer, *Plato*, 192; and Keulen, *Untersuchungen*, 51). But surely all this is very strange. In a hymnic recitation of ages, we are told, Euthydemus celebrates a major doctrine of Plato—and the doctrine, perhaps, is here made public for the first time. But why would Plato present this important doctrine in a "hollow" (or crazed) "hymnic recitation"—which is directed against Socrates, who will soon become the doctrine's chief spokesman? It is surely inadequate to say (with Hawtrey) that Plato is merely "enjoying" himself (see note 14 below).

11. Concerning Socrates's exclamation *polytimete Euthydeme*, Hawtrey comments that "the adjective [*polytimete*], here of course used in irony, is normally used of gods;" and there are several other passages (288a, 273e, 296d), all noted by Hawtrey, in which the brothers are addressed in a manner suited to divinities (*Commentary*, 156). Gifford, too, finds this mode of address striking, and he even goes so far as to suggest that the proper reply to those who find the Euthydemus frivolous is that Plato represents Socrates as "pretending to marvel at [the brothers'] supernatural wisdom, and even to address them as absolutely divine" (*The Euthydemus of Plato*, 11)—though Gifford doesn't make it clear why a merely ironic use of names reserved for divinity should reassure, rather than alarm, those who find the *Euthydemus* frivolous.

5. Boundless Truth

> But tell me, I went on, how am I to say I know certain things, Euthydemus, such as, for example, that the good are unrighteous. Come, tell me, do I know this or not?
>
> Of course, you know it, he said.
>
> Know what? I said.
>
> That the good are not unrighteous.
>
> Yes, I said, I knew that all along. But that's not what I'm asking. I'm asking where I have learned that the good are unrighteous.
>
> Nowhere, said Dionysodorus.
>
> Then I do not know this, I said.
>
> You are spoiling the argument, said Euthydemus to Dionysodorus.
>
> Dionysodorus reddened. (296e–297a)

Let us first consider the issue that Socrates has raised. The ordinary mind—the mind unenlightened by the brothers—can easily know, for example, that 2 x 2 = 4, because the objective nature of number dictates this bit of knowledge. But the ordinary mind can get no further with 2 x 2. To the question of 2 x 2, only one solution is conceivable; all other solutions are denied. Such, then, is the ordinary mind. Now, what of the ecstatic mind, the mind that the brothers have enlightened?

Of course the ecstatic mind knows that 2 x 2 = 4; almost any human being can get as far as that. But the ecstatic mind also knows that 2 x 2 = 5. For if the ecstatic mind knows "all things"—and the brothers assure us that it does—then the five to be obtained by the multiplication of two by two cannot, for a moment, be withheld from it.

In fact, the ecstatic mind knows an infinite number of things that other minds find unintelligible. The oddness of twelve, the evenness of seven, the snow hotter than fire, the fire colder than snow, the time that flows backwards, the whole smaller than its part—all this the ecstatic mind knows.

But how can such knowledge be possible? In order to answer the question, we turn to a text that must have exceptional value for us, since it appears to be a fragment of the "real" Euthydemus, the historical sophist who lived at the time of Socrates. Plato himself preserves this fragment in the *Cratylus* (386d). The fragment reads as follows: *pasi panta homoios...hama kai aei*—All are equally in all...simultaneously and forever.[12]

Now if it is true, as Euthydemus teaches, that all dwell equally in all, then "fiveness" dwells in two twos to the same degree as "fourness," and heat dwells within snow to the same degree as coldness, and oddness dwells in twelve to the same degree as evenness, and so on in all other cases. So the objective nature of truth cannot constrain the mind enlightened by Euthydemus, because the dwelling of all in all disclosed by Euthydemus confers truth on every positive claim.

Here, then, we discern the ground of the omniscience which the brothers offer Socrates. There is no structure to truth; truth is formless and dark. So Socrates, too, can know a state which is formless and dark—a state which is therefore one with truth. And what is it like, this state which is one with truth?

As it begins to stir within Socrates, it has something of the aura of evil desires and dreams.[13] This explains why Socrates's question about it has the particular content it has. "Come, he asks, "tell me...where have I learned that the good are unrighteous? (297a)"

Now, for the ordinary mind, goodness excludes unrighteousness the way snow excludes heat and eight excludes oddness. But

---

12. In his translation of the *Cratylus*, Fowler offers the following note on the *pasi panta homoios*, which Socrates, at 386d, attributes to Euthydemus: "The doctrine here attributed to Euthydemus is not expressly enunciated by him in the dialogue which bears his name, but it is little more than a comprehensive statement of the several doctrines there proclaimed by him and his brother Dionysodorus," *Plato IV: Cratylus, Parmenides, Greater Hippias, Lesser Hippias*, trans. H. N. Fowler, Loeb Classical Library 167 (Cambridge: Harvard University Press, 1926), ix).

13. In the *Cratylus*, too, Socrates makes it clear that the *pasi panta homoios* leads "beyond" good and evil (386d).

for the mind enlightened by the brothers, "all dwell equally in all," so unrighteousness dwells impartially in good and evil alike. But why does Dionysodorus give the surprising answer of "nowhere" when Socrates asks where he has learned that the good are unrighteous?

The reason, of course, is that there never was a moment and never was a place where Socrates actually acquired this piece of knowledge. He did not have to acquire it, for he has never ceased to possess it. He has known it from before the dawn of time (296d).[14]

But this timeless knowledge is hidden, and the brothers want to set it free. And Socrates, for his part, though "minded to take lessons from this new teacher (295d)," still feels tempted to flee.

6. Between Beasts

> You know, gentlemen, I am weaker than either one of you, and it's right that I should run from the two of you together. You see, I am sadly inferior to Hercules, who was unable, all alone, to contend against the hydra—this hydra being in actual fact a sophist, and so clever a sophist, too, that if you cut off the head of a single one of her arguments, she grew many more such heads to replace the one she had lost; so even Hercules, I say, was no match for the hydra; at least not when she was joined by a certain sophistical crab, just now emerged from the sea, I should think, and freshly arrived on our shore, and whose leftward talking and snapping so troubled the hero that he cried out, finally, for help from his nephew Iolaus, and Iolaus helped him effectively. (297c)

This is a striking image. The hydra is so constituted that, when you cut off one of her heads, many heads emerge to replace it. There is thus always more to the hydra, and the principle of boundlessness, which is the theme of the brothers' instruction, is plainly represented by this beast.

---

14. The other possibility is that Dionysodorus cannot bear to make the admission that "the good are unjust," because it sounds so immoral. But why should this worry him, when he speaks so cheerfully of murdering youths, and so on?

Hercules, moreover, is caught between two dangers—the hydra on the right, the crab on the left. If Iolaus now joins Hercules, then the arrangement of heros and monsters in the story will remind us of the arrangement of pupils and teachers in our text—an arrangement described at 271b:

Hydra/Hercules/Iolaus/Crab

Euthydemus/Cleinias/Socrates/Dionysodorus

One thinks, too, of the *Parmenides* of Plato, where two principles of boundlessness (= the monsters = the brothers) "sandwich in" two realms of structured being (= Hercules and Iolaus = Socrates and Cleinias). In the *Parmenides*, the arrangement is like this:

BOUNDLESSNESS	BOUNDARIES	BOUNDARIES	BOUNDLESSNESS
The One without the Others	The One with the Others	The Others with the One	The Others without the One

But let us return to Hercules and Iolaus.

Plato, it seems, was drawn to Hercules and Iolaus; and he recalls them again in an important text in the *Phaedo*. There, the two "monsters" are Simmias and Cebes, and they are trying to frighten the heroes, Socrates and Phaedo, with their pessimistic attitude toward death. Socrates, however, whose hour of death has come, enters the struggle fearlessly, and rallies his comrade as follows:

> I would take an oath, Phaedo, and not let my hair grow again, until I had...defeated the arguments of Sirnmias and Cebes.
>
> But you know what they say, Socrates. Not even Hercules was a match for two.
>
> Why, then, call upon me to help as your Iolaus—call while their is still light.
>
> I call upon you, indeed, sir, but as Iolaus calling to Hercules. (89c)

Socrates, dying, defeats the "monsters" Simmias and Cebes and then passes magnificently into the Other World. Thus two crushing obstacles—in the guise of two youths—form a gateway to the Other World.

Of course there are many such gateways, and in the text cited below, we encounter again such a gateway—a gateway, this time, through which all of us have passed. I am speaking, of course, of our parents.

7. *The Father*

> Tell me, Socrates, said Dionysodorus, is Patrocles your brother?
>
> Certainly, I said—that is, by the same mother, but not by the same father. His father is Chaeredemus, mine Sophronicus.
>
> So Sophronicus and Chaeredemus are both "father?"
>
> Yes, I said, the former mine, the latter his.
>
> Then, surely, he continued, Chaeredemus is other than a father?
>
> Than mine, at least, I said.
>
> Therefore, he is a father, while being other than a father. But are you the same as—stone?
>
> I'm afraid, I said, that you will prove that of me, but I must tell you, I do not feel like it.
>
> Then you are other than stone?
>
> Other, yes, I confess it.
>
> And being other than stone means not being stone? And being other than gold means not being gold?
>
> Certainly, I said.
>
> And therefore Chaeredemus, being other than a father, cannot, it seems, be "father."
>
> Evidently he is not a father, I said.
>
> That's right, said Euthydemus, taking up the argument, for if Chaeredemus is a father, then Sophronicus, I would think, being other than a father, couldn't be a father at all—so that you, Socrates, are fatherless (298a–298b).

Let us begin by discussing the overarching principle on which the argument just quoted is based. If, says Euthydemus, you are other than gold, then you are not gold. And if you are other than stone, then you are not stone (298a).[15] Now Socrates agrees with these assertions—but what does his agreement imply?

Suppose I look at my ring, which happens to be made of gold. Now, if my ring were other than gold, then, of course, it would not be gold—so I must understand that there can be no gold, anywhere in the world, which is other than the gold of my ring. What, then, do I see in my ring? I see gold, boundless gold—the whole world insofar as it is gold.

Likewise, every stone is the substance of all stone, every fire is the substance of all fire. The blue of this patch of sky is all the blue in the world, and the beauty of these hills is all the beauty in the world. I will never find in the world the slightest trace of a quality which does not, rightly viewed, contain within itself every possible instance of itself, for it cannot be cut off from what it is. But the particular boundless object of which the brothers wish to speak is, first of all the father. It seems that, if Socrates's father is not the

---

15. In her translation of the *Euthydemus*, Sprague comments: "This whole series of arguments involving 'same,' 'other,' and 'not' should certainly be studied in connection with the analysis of negation in 'The Sophist'" (*Plato: Euthydemus*, 49, n. 78). Hawtrey plainly agrees: "This is, I believe, the first passage in which Plato (in the mouth here, with typical paradox, of one of the Sophists) uses the term *heteros* to explain what might be called a kind of non-being" (*Commentary*, 166). For my part, as I have already indicated, I am trying to explain the "typical paradox" mentioned by Hawtrey—that so much of value in Platonism is introduced in the brothers' discourse. If I am offered the explanation that Plato is simply "enjoying" himself, I will reply that anything in literature—absolutely anything, however striking or strange or heavy with portentous significance—might be passed over lightly and thus not examined at all with just this sort of remark. Now, I want to concede at once that authors frequently "enjoy" themselves, and they do this, at times, in strange and troubling ways. But the question ought always to arise as to why an author has enjoyed himself (or herself) in the particular way he (she) has chosen, and with regard to the *Euthydemus* (where the manner of enjoyment is surely astonishing), this question must be pressed home (see note 20).

father of Chaeredemus, then Socrates's father is other than a father and so not a father at all.

All philosophers, as Plato suggests in the *Sophist*, have patricidal tendencies (241d). "You, Socrates, are fatherless," as Euthydemus sternly declares. But the other possibility is that Socrates has a father, and all creatures have fathers, and the father of one is the father of all, on pain of being other than a father. This is the view that Euthydemus now advances, for he aims to disclose the boundless mother and father through whom the boundless soul is born.

8. Boundless Parents

> Here Ctesippus took up the argument and said: But tell us, Euthydemus, about your own father. Isn't he other than my father?
>
> Not at all, he said.
>
> The same, then?—I would not like to think it! But tell me, he said, is he my father only, or is he everyone else's too?
>
> Everyone else's too, he said.
>
> Well, is he the father of humans only, or of horses, too, and other beasts?
>
> Of all, he said.
>
> And is your mother a mother in the same way?
>
> Yes, my mother too.
>
> And is your mother a mother of sea urchins?
>
> Yes, and yours is too, he said.
>
> Then you are a brother of piglets, gudgeons, and puppy dogs?
>
> Yes, and so are you, he said. (298c–e)

This strikes us, perhaps, as the stupidest text in the dialogue, and certainly we are reminded of exchanges that go on between children, who seem to take pleasure in addressing one another in this way. "You are a pig!" says one child. "And so are you!" says the other. "Your father's a pig!" says a child. "And so is yours!" says the other. This goes on for many minutes as the children laugh uncontrollably. But apart from reminding us of the giddy behavior of children, our text has a meaning that, roughly, is this: just as every soul, viewed as a bounded psychic entity, has a set of bounded parents, so the boundless soul—the soul disclosed by the brothers—has a set of boundless parents from whom it takes its life.[16]

How can we find our boundless parents? We must reason, it seems, like this: just as all the world's gold can be found in every bit of gold, and all the world's stone can be found in every bit of stone, so, too, the boundless parents can be found in our own parents. We have only to notice that, since our parents really are parents, the substance of their "parentness" cannot be other than any other parent's. So their limits fade. Their "parentness" swells and expands, and soon they are parents of rodents, lizards, bugs and all other beasts, so that the beasts are our sisters and brothers.

It seems, then, that the apprehension of boundless parents is connected to the experience of intimacy with beasts, which is a well-known theme in the world of mythology. The lost paradise where humans talked to beasts, the shaman with animal familiars, the hero raised by beasts, the hunter who prays to the beasts he hunts—Eliade, among others, has discussed these themes.[17]

Nor is this intimacy with beasts merely a theme of myth. It is also, in some sense, a fact of human experience. Consider, for example, the charmers of spiders and snakes, of whom Socrates speaks at

---

16. James Hillman writes: "The belief that parents shape my world from the beginning strikes me as a variety of 'misplaced concreteness.' I take the term from the English philosopher Alfred North Whitehead. Misplaced concreteness does not keep 'abstract' and 'concrete' distinct enough. Cosmic mythical parents and personal mothers and fathers get mixed up. Then the formative powers and mysteries assigned to abstractions such as heaven and earth, Sky God and Earth Goddess (or vice versa, in Egyptian myth) become concrete mothers and fathers, while mothers and fathers are divinized, causing effects of cosmic proportions," *The Soul's Code: In Search of Character and Calling* (New York: HarperCollins, 1996), 85.

17. See, for example, *Shamanism: Archaic Techniques of Ecstasy*, trans. Willard Trask (Princeton, N.J.: Princeton University Press, 1974), *passim*.

289e in our text; presumably they have obtained an intimacy with beasts. Then, too—and for us this is most pertinent—Dionysian ecstasy seemed to restore the fullness of the intimacy. Thus the Maenads danced with beasts, nursed small animals, and crowned their heads and wrapped their waists with poisonous snakes over which they had power.[18]

It seems, too, that Plato must have experienced something of the intimacy with animals or at least understood the idea of it. Certainly he surprises many of his admirers by informing them that their souls may one day enter the bodies of beasts. He declares that sentient life, human as well as bestial, has a single origin and destiny—the realm of soul described in the *Phaedrus* (247d–249e).

However, it is true that the "intimacy with beasts" described by the brothers veers quickly in a most unpleasant direction, and the following joke, hard to surpass in obscenity, escapes Dionysodorus's lips.

9. Dionysodorus's Joke

> Just tell me, Ctesippus, have you a dog?
>
> Yes, a real rogue.
>
> And has he pups?
>
> Yes, a set of rogues like him.
>
> Then, is the dog their father?
>
> Yes, I saw him with my own eyes, covering the bitch.
>
> Then he is a father and yours, and so—a dog is your father! You are the brother of whelps! And one point more: do you beat this dog?
>
> God, yes! Since I can't beat you…
>
> Why, then, you beat your father! (298d–e)

---

18. Euripides, *The Bacchae*, 665–705.

This absurd joke,[19] in which one beats one's "own" father, having observed him "covering a bitch," combines voyeurism, sadism, outrage, bestiality, and other obscure transgressions, hard to define or name. Even here, however, there is perhaps a religious horizon. The "vision" of parents copulating must be linked to the moment in which the discarnate soul enters a new worldly life. In *The Tibetan Book of the Dead* (*Bardo Thödol*), these events are connected explicitly. As for the "beating of the father," the Greek imagination was somehow haunted by the thought of it. Aristophanes used to joke about it—and with special reference to Socrates;[20] and Hesiod's *Theogony* is, in a way, a story of "father-beating," for Uranus is conquered by Cronos, who is conquered by Zeus in turn.

At any rate, the ghastly joke of Dionysodorus concludes the discussion of parents. It now comes about that, through the boundless parents, we enter a boundless world. Our first boundless object is—a drug.[21]

10. Boundless Drugs

> I don't suppose, Euthydemus, Ctesippus inquired, that your particular brand of wisdom has done your father much good?

---

19. "The charm of this argument," Chance writes, "even cast its spell on Aristotle, who incorporated it into his *Sophisti Elenchi*…and subsequently this sophism has passed into logic handbooks as a permanent model by which Aristotelians illustrate what they call the fallacy or accident" (163). May I add that the content of the argument—with its Oedipal resentment and mystical baggage—has something to do with its curious persistence?

20. Aristophanes, *The Clouds*, 395.

21. The "expansive" images in this part of the dialogue include: a boundless father (298*c*), a boundless mother (298*d*), a drug that grows (299*b*), a man that grows (299*c*), a warrior whose limbs are legion (299*d*), and a bit of gold that spreads all over the world, covering and penetrating everything (299*e*). Now, when strikingly juxtaposed images are transparently homologous, there is likely to be a reason—and in this case the meaning is obvious. The common element here is expansiveness, and we know (from reports in Aristotle) that Plato often spoke of an ultimate power of expansiveness—the "dyad" or "great-and-small" (See 134).

He doesn't need much good, Euthydemus replied, and for that matter, neither do you.[22]

And what about you, Euthydemus? asked Ctesippus. Do you need much good?

Not at all, he said; and neither does anyone else. But come, now, Ctesippus, and answer what I ask: when sick or feeble people take the drugs they require, do you find that good or not good?

Good, said Ctesippus. But I think you will now say something witty.

You'll see if I do, Euthydemus replied; however, you must answer this: since drugs, as you say, are good to drink when necessary, will it not be necessary to drink this good as much as possible? And will not the effect be particularly fine if a cart load of hellebore is pounded out and added to it?

That's true, Ctesippus replied, if your drinker's as big as the Delphian statue! (299*b–c*)

Ctesippus, then, is asked to envision a drug. Now, the drug, he agrees, is good, if one takes it only when necessary. The drug, in other words, is good, if it is used within proper limits.

It seems, however, that as soon as Ctesippus agrees that the drug is good when it is used within proper limits, he is directed to envision the unlimited use of the drug. Thus the dose, in effect, starts to grow—one swallows as much of it as possible. And soon the dose to be taken has in fact become so immense that a whole cart load

---

22. Of Euthydemus's claim that *ouden deita pollon agathon,* Hawtrey writes: "There is again a sense in which the sophist speaks a Platonic truth: no one needs a lot of good things because there is really only one good thing, namely wisdom." But "it is difficult to say," adds Hawtrey, "why Plato puts his own doctrines in the despised mouths of Euthydemus and Dionysodorus; I am inclined to suspect that he is enjoying himself and entertaining his more intelligent readers." But this cannot be the whole explanation. For the "despised" figures who have here become Plato's spokesmen present images as horrific as any in classical literature. The question must arise as to why it would be "entertaining"—rather than crazy or tasteless—to cause such figures as these to present doctrines one cherished.

of Hellebore—which was typically used as a purgative—must be pounded out and added to it.

But why does the drug keep "growing" in this way? This is the explanation: the drug is said to be good—it is good, at least, within limits. But if, as Ctesippus thinks, people "need lots of good," then, Euthydemus points out, what is good in limited measure should be better when the limits are removed, for then lots of good is given to us.[23] Euthydemus, then, has created a situation where there is no such thing as a limited human desire. For desire is always of the good, and we always need lots of good. Desire, therefore, is expansive—it craves ever greater doses of the good that its object contains.

Now, how does Ctesippus respond to this movement of expansion? Ctesippus, in fact, is pleased by it. Ctesippus seems to "become Corybantic" at the moment when he laughs at the joke about beating his father (298e).[24] If he still feels inclined to dispute with the brothers, it is not any longer to resist their propositions but in order to go further than they.

To be sure, then, there is a drug, and the drug has been found to be good, and the doses to be taken have been growing at a rapid rate. But it is right, Ctesippus adds, that the doses of the drug should grow in this way because the user of the drug is growing in just the same way. The user, indeed, is now as big as the statue at Delphi,

---

23. Of the drug, Sprague writes: "This is a *dicto simpliciter ad dictum secundum quid*; what is good is good absolutely is said to be good in some particular ridiculous way," *Plato's Use of Fallacy*, 25.

24. Perhaps this assault on the father is demanded by the goddess who has started drawing near. Hillman writes: "The ecstatic aspect in a man...takes him further from the father's inhibitions of order and limit. Ecstasy is one of the goddess's ways of seducing the puer from its senex connection. By overcoming limit, puer consciousness feels itself overcoming fate," "The Great Mother, Her Son, Her Hero, and the Puer" in *Fathers and Mothers: Five Papers on the Archetypal Background of Family Psychology*, ed. Patricia Berry (New York and Zurich: Spring Publications, 1973), 86. Reprinted in *Uniform Edition of the Writings of James Hillman*, vol. 3: *Senex and Puer*.

and can drink as much as he desires, for the drug makes him equal to his need.

11. *The Many-Limbed Warrior*

> Then, too, said Euthydemus, since in war it's good to carry weapons, it will be necessary to carry as many spears and shields as possible, since weapons, we agree, are a good thing.
>
> Yes, I think so, answered Ctesippus. But do you Euthydemus, wish to deny this view, and say that one spear and shield would be best?
>
> I do.
>
> Ah, but would you arm Geryon in this way, and would you so arm Briareus? I thought, Euthydemus, that you were more an expert than that, considering you're an old soldier, and your comrade here, too.
>
> At this Euthydemus fell silent. (299c)

Ctesippus, then, is asked to envision a drug. Now, the drug, he agrees, is good, if one takes it only when necessary. The drug, in other words, is good, if it is used within proper limits.

Will not the warrior be crushed beneath these weapons? Certainly, this is to be feared. But here, once again, the seduced or hypnotized Ctesippus is pleased by the image that Euthydemus shows him and he completes and perfects this image. It is good, Ctesippus says, that the warrior's weapons have doubled and redoubled, for the limbs of the warrior have likewise doubled and redoubled. Thus the warrior is Geryon, the six-armed giant. Or the warrior is Briareus, the hundred-armed giant.

12. *Boundless Gold*

> Dionysodorus now raised some questions concerning Ctesippus's previous replies. Is it right, he began, to have good things always and everywhere?
>
> Yes, he replied.
>
> And you agree, do you not, that gold is a good thing?
>
> I do, he said.

> Why then, we ought always to have it, and everywhere, and above all in ourselves. So we shall be happiest if three talents of gold are stuffed in our belly, and a talent in our skull, and a stater in each of our eyes.
>
> You are right, sir! You are right! For the happiest men in Skythia, they say, have vast amounts of gold in their "own" skulls...and a still more marvelous thing is told, how they drink from their skulls when gilded, and how they gaze inside them, holding them in their hands. (299d–e)

Let us speak, first, of the gold. What is the value of gold? In the *Hippias Major* (at 289e), a theory is proposed in which the value of gold must rise beyond all measure for the simple reason that gold is beauty itself. Thus the beauty of an object would increase in proportion to its gold, and the vision of pure beauty (which is the aim of love and philosophy) would be simply a vision of gold; boundless gold in its purest state.

Turning back to the *Euthydemus*, we find that it contains several references to gold. It is implied at 298a that the smallest portion of gold contains all the world's gold, and we read at 289a of turning the world to gold, an achievement somehow connected with the obtaining of boundless life (289b). But the most important reference to gold comes near the end of the dialogue where Socrates speaks his parting words to the brothers. These parting words (to be discussed later) allude to a verse of Pindar, in which water (prime matter) is said, of all things, to be best, but gold (matter perfected) is, in another way, also best, blazing out like a fire in the night.

> Best of all things is water, but gold,
> Like a blazing fire, by night outshines all pride
> of wealth beside.[25]

What, then, is gold? It is beauty, immortality, transcendence. This reminds us of alchemy, which would emerge as a "science" several centuries after Alexander the Great, and among whose most important predecessors we may certainly count the secret society

---

25. *Odes of Pindar*, trans. Richmond Lattimore (Chicago: The University of Chicago Press, 1976).

of the Corybantes—a society which combined an art of refining metals with a mystical practice of scope and depth.[26]

Now we arrive at a curious fact. When Dionysodorus proposes that the world turn to gold, the image of a skull obtrudes into the discussion. This skull is filled with gold, and its eyes are pierced with gold. Though gold certainly signifies transcendence, beauty, and immortality, it would yet seem to be the most dangerous of metals for whoever has the temerity to seek boundless gold must perish—horribly dismembered—in the superabundance sought (299e).

Now, does this frighten Ctesippus? It does not in the least frighten Ctesippus. In fact there now arises in the enchanted mind of Ctesippus the radiant image of a miraculous human being who could survive the ordeal just described by Dionysodorus.

Yet, who is this fabulous being? This being, it seems, is a Skythian. For the Skythians took the heads of enemies whom they had slain in battle, and made cups from the skulls, and gilded the inside surface.[27] Ctesippus, speaking of the Skythians, has only to quibble on the possessive pronoun *heautou* ("their own") to produce just the image he needs.

---

26. Regarding the emergence of alchemy, see Eliade, *The Forge and the Crucible*, 77–78. "In alchemy," Hillman writes, "we find pathologizing as an integral, necessary aspect of soul-making...So much is this the case that when we enter the thought of alchemy, these events lose their stigma of sickness and become metaphors for necessary phases of the soul-making process. So we find: processes of dismemberment, torture, cannibalism, decapitation, flaying, poisoning; images of monsters, dragons, unipeds, skeletons, hermaphrodites; operations called putrefaction, mortification, pulverizing, dissolution," James Hillman, *Re-Visioning Psychology* (New York: Harper & Row, 1975), 90.

27. Herodotus writes as follows: "As regards war, the Scythian custom is for every man to drink the blood of the first man he kills. The heads of all the enemies killed in battle are taken to the king...they have a special way of dealing with the actual skulls—not with all of them, but only those of their worst enemies: they saw off the part below the eye-brows and after cleaning out what remains, stretch a piece of rawhide round it on the outside. If a man is poor, he is content with that, but a rich man goes further and gilds the inside of the skull as well. In either case the skull is used to drink from," *Histories*, 4.65 (trans. Aubrey de Selincourt).

> The happiest men in Skythia, they say, have vast amounts of gold in their "own" skulls and a still more marvelous thing is told, how they drink from their skulls when gilded, and how they gaze inside them, holding them in their hands. (299d–e)[28]

Whoever desires boundless gold must be cut into parts and filled with gold. But the Skythian, it seems, can survive this ordeal—it makes him "most happy."

All of these themes are familiar to the history of religion. The alchemist, for example, who turns the world to gold, may frequently contemplate his "own" hollow skull—the cup, made from a skull, which he uses for mixing drugs. The experience of decapitation, of having one's body stuffed with esoteric matter, of seeing one's body as if from a distance, of seeing one's own bones—all this belongs to the visionary practice of not only Inuit shamanism[29] but also of Western occultism. But what is the connection between the power to make gold and submission to terrible ordeals?

Perhaps the explanation is that whoever desires to make gold (or desires, in general, the power to dominate matter) must first obtain spiritual perfection, and spiritual perfection is achieved only through suffering—through symbolic dismemberment and death. But maybe, after all, the most important feature of the image constructed by Ctesippus is that it leads us beyond the subject-object dichotomy. For the Skythian, it seems, has an object in his hand, but the object is the subject—the skull of the subject himself.

---

28. For modern readers, the most famous image of a man contemplating a skull—a skull with which he seems to identify, though it is not strictly his "own"—is that of Hamlet at Ophelia's grave, with the skull of Yorick in his hand. In this connection, let us recall Hawtrey's admirable comparison between the brothers and Rosencrantz and Guildenstern (92, n. 3); and let us note as well that Crito's relation to Socrates resembles Hamlet's relation to Horatio—it is that of a death-haunted genius to his "normal," loyal friend. Then, too, a ghost initiates Hamlet's adventure; a daimon initiates Socrates's.

29. See Eliade, *Shamanism*, 45, 47–50, *passim*.

13. *Vision and the Visible*

> Tell me, said Euthydemus, do Skythians and men in general see things capable of sight, or incapable.
>
> Capable, I presume.
>
> And you, too?
>
> I, too.
>
> Do you see our cloaks, then?
>
> To be sure.
>
> Are they capable of sight?
>
> Quite extraordinarily.
>
> What do they see?
>
> Nothing. But I think perhaps you don't believe the cloaks can see—you are such a sweet innocent. I'd say, Euthydemus, that you are sleeping without going to sleep, and if it be possible to speak and say or describe Nothing, that is what you are doing here. (300a–b)

The phrase *dunata horan* has, of course, a double meaning—it means "able to see" and "possible to see." Now "able to see" describes the subject of vision, while "possible to see" describes the object of vision—in the phrase *dunata horan*, the subject and object rise as one.[30]

Euthydemus, then, taking up the phrase *dunata horan*, suggests to Ctesippus that, if he considers the world with sufficient penetration, he will find that his power to see is the same as the power of objects to be seen. He will find, in other words, that vision and the visible are one. Thus the earth can see, the sky can see, and all

---

30. Here we arrive at a new kind of equivocation, one based on syntax rather than diction—and before us looms an interesting series of jokes, where the grammatical subject and object merge in an ambiguous way. Previous commentators, as a rule, have discussed only the form of the joke, but is it too much to point out that, when a mystical philosopher like Plato achieves by means of a joke a union of subject and object, there is likely to be a hidden meaning—and especially if the joke involves "vision?" For almost every kind of mysticism is based upon a vision where subject and object become one.

things can see exactly insofar as they are seen. And the sun that gives light to the earth, the sky, and all things—the sun sees what it shines on pre-eminently.

"O ray of sun,/much seeing mother of the eyes..." These lines from Pindar (fr. 44), which remind us, to be sure, of Plato's own discussion of the sun in the *Republic* (Book Seven), are like a sublime rendition of Euthydemus's "stupid" joke, in which the cloaks, being seen, can see.

And what is the outcome of the joke? The outcome is very peculiar. It seems that, when Euthydemus says that the cloaks are "able to see," the increasingly "Corybantic" Ctesippus feels an overwhelming impulse to accept what he has been told. And yet Ctesippus has the impression—a giddy, slightly anxious impression—that the brothers do not themselves believe it when they speak to him about the cloaks, but are trying to raise him to an intensely "Corybantic" state which they cannot (or do not wish to) share. Of course, the cloaks can see—they can "quite extraordinarily."[31] "But," says Ctesippus looking suspiciously at Euthydemus, "I think perhaps you don't believe the cloaks can see—you are such a sweet innocent" (300*a*).

"You are sleeping," Ctesippus adds—and here he advances further into the state he is experiencing—"without going to sleep. (300*b*)." But why is sleep referred to in this place?

In fact, the rites of the Corybantes, on which the brothers base their performances, were linked in ancient times to a condition connected with sleep—thus Pliny was under the impression that the verb *korabantein* ("to become Corybantic") referred to a condition in which one slept "with eyes open" (*patentibus dormiunt*).[32] Now to sleep "with eyes open" is in a way to sleep "without going to sleep." But what does sleeping "with eyes open" have to do with the Corybantic rites?

---

31. I feel sure that Sprague is right when she tells us that the brothers must be wearing very peculiar cloaks—cloaks that, as Ctesippus says, come into view "extraordinarily," *Plato: Euthydemus*, 151.

32. Pliny, *Natural History*, 11.37, 54, 147.

Perhaps, as some have suggested,[33] there was in ancient times a nervous disorder, thought to be caused by the Corybantes, of which one of the symptoms was literally "sleeping with eyes open." One can easily envision someone suffering this disorder. He would be sound asleep but would stare into space with empty eyes.

There is, however, another possible explanation—which, as we shall see, our text tends to support. We should note that certain supernormal states of mind are described in mystical literature as "remaining conscious while asleep" or "being conscious of sleep."[34] Now, the point of this designation is that, when we fall asleep, we are released from individuality and absorbed, more or less, by the Undifferentiated. So if we are conscious of being asleep—if we "sleep with eyes open" or "sleep without sleeping"—we shall obtain the transcendence we desire. Almost certainly Plato took an interest in this phenomenon. That is why, in the *Apology*, when Socrates speaks of death as a dreamless sleep, he assures us that the prospect, far from discouraging him, fills him with longing and joy (25*d*).

But what is it one sees in that wakeful sleep without dreams? What is it one sees, when one learns to "sleep without sleeping?" A one-word answer to the question is given twice in the text, smuggled in, as it were, in the discourse of Ctesippus. Sleeping without sleeping one sees "Nothing," and "if," Ctesippus says, "it be possible...to speak and say or describe 'Nothing,' that is what you are doing here."

That the ultimate mystical object should present itself as "Nothing" is suggested more or less directly in the later dialogues of Plato. Thus, the Good in the *Republic* is beyond essence and being. The One in the *Parmenides* is entirely without being. Many thinkers—Plotinus, Dionysus, Eckhart, Ruysbroeck, Hegel, Heidegger,

---

33. This is Linforth's explanation in "Corybantic Rites in Plato," 1155.

34. This is a recurrent doctrine in the principle Upanishads. Eliade's treatment of it in his fictional work, "The Secret of Dr. Honigberger," in *Two Tales of the Occult*, trans. William Ames Coates (New York: Herder and Herder, 1970), seems to me particularly illuminating—though intentionally somewhat fantastic.

Sartre, and others—have felt the impact of Plato's remarks in which ultimate transcendence is vacuity.

Of course, the brothers seemed to eliminate "that-which-is-not" in the second part of their discourse (284*b*, 286*a*), but there they were operating on a much lower plane. For assuredly some sort of nothingness is seeping into their discourse. We will "hear" this nothingness in the text cited below as a silence that is capable of speech.

14. *The Speaking of the Silent*

> What? asked Dionysodorus. May there not be a speaking of the silent?
>
> By no means whatever, replied Ctesippus.
>
> Or a silence of the speaking?
>
> Still less.
>
> But what if you speak of stones and timbers and irons—is that not speaking of the silent?
>
> Not if I walk by a smithy, Ctesippus replied; for here, as they say, the irons speak and cry aloud, when they are touched. And so, my friend, you're saying Nothing and don't know it—and doing it just because you're wise.
>
> Ctesippus, it seemed, was excited because of his friend. (300*c*)

Let us consider, first of all, the phrase "the speaking of the silent" to which Ctesippus is now introduced. The Greek phrase here is *sigonta legein*, where *sigonta* ("silent things") functions simultaneously as the subject and the object of *legein* ("to speak"). An aim of the brothers' discourse is that the subject and object rise as one, and here this aim is achieved by the syntactical role of *sigonta*, just as it was achieved by *ta dunata horan*.

Now let us think for a moment about "the speaking of the silent." If snow covers the ground, and you "listen" to the snow, you "hear" a kind of silence, or if you climb a mountain and "listen" to the sky, you again "hear" a kind of silence. This kind of silence is more than the absence of sound. It is itself a kind of sound, the most perfect, most stirring sound—exactly a "speaking of the silent."[35]

Ctesippus, however, dislikes the "speaking of the silent." Ctesippus, to be sure, has grown giddy and will accept many doctrines that may fairly be called outrageous, but he is annoyed, all the same, by the phrase "to be silent." It does not seem to him that silent things are possible at all. For Dionysodorus has foolishly suggested that "stones and timbers and irons" are silent—but it is clear that these things speak. Irons, in particular, speak. For "if I walk by a smithy, the irons speak and cry aloud."

Now, why is it that a smithy obtrudes itself in this place? As a matter of fact, the society of the Corybantes was precisely a society of smiths, and the mythical Corybantes were said to be the first smiths. So any attempt to portray the rites of the Corybantes must speak of a smithy. But why does Ctesippus say that the irons being worked on "speak and cry aloud when they are touched," as if the smith tormented human beings, rather than working on metals?

As a matter of fact (as Eliade shows), in myths all over the world, the art of the smith is founded by means of a sacrifice.[36] We have already spoken of a myth concerning the Dactyloi (= the Corybantes) that could perhaps describe an act of this sort. Here the original smiths are Akmon and Damnameneus, or "Anvil" and

---

35. As for properly mystical silence, there are of course countless descriptions, but the most famous, perhaps, is to be found in Augustine's *Confessions*. I will cite the text here, in case the reader finds it helpful, fully aware of the incongruity between Augustine's lyricism and the brothers' convoluted jests. "If for any man the tumult of the flesh grew silent, silent the images of earth, sea, and air; if the heavens grew silent...and the soul itself grew silent...if all dreams and imaginative visions and every tongue and every sign and all that is transient grew silent...and God alone should speak to us...would not this be what is meant by the words—'Enter into the joy of your Lord'" (*Confessions*, IX.X). Concerning Augustine, Narcy reports the view that Socrates's exhortations in the *Euthydemus* exerted, through the mediation of Aristotle, an influence on Cicero's *Hortensius*, the work that inspired Augustine to take up philosophy (*Le Philosophe et son double*, 28). It is possible, though it seems fantastic, that we owe Augustine to Euthydemus.

36. On the role of sacrifice in the origin of metallurgy, see Eliade, *The Forge and the Crucible*, 62–70, *passim*.

"the Compeller." They crush their brother between them; Kelmis (the knife).

We know that the role of the murdered Kelmis is played in our dialogue by Cleinias. Thus, the "irons" that "speak and cry aloud when they are touched" can be none other than Cleinias, and this explains why, when Ctesippus speaks of the irons, Socrates immediately recalls the presence of Cleinias; Cleinias who has said nothing in the course of the brothers' discourse since the moment of his "death" at 283d.

15. *The Silence of the Speaking*

> But, said Ctesippus, you must now propound your other point, that there can be a silence of the speaking.
>
> When you are silent, said Euthydemus, are you not making silence of all things?
>
> Yes, he said.
>
> Then, the speaking, too, are silent, my dear man, if the speaking belong among all things. (300c)

The exact opposite of "the speaking of the silent" is "the silence of the speaking." And "the silence of the speaking" is obtained from certain words that the brothers here pronounce to Ctesippus—the words *panta sigas*. *Panta sigas* means, "you are silent concerning all things."

Panta sigas also and equally means, "you cause all things to be silent." Suppose, then, that thunder crashes, or swords clash, or there is music, shouting, and laughter. Suppose that we, hearing these things, preserve a silence concerning them. We then have *panta sigas* in the sense that we ourselves are silent. But suddenly there occurs the subject-object transposition to which the brothers, with their joke, call attention. We are silent in the face of that which sounds, and then suddenly our silence encloses that which sounds, pervades that which sounds. Thunder crashes, swords clash, the laughter swells to a maximum, but all are enclosed within spheres of silence, the way figures in Japanese painting are enclosed within empty space.

But now we arrive at a serious disagreement between Ctesippus and the brothers, and Ctesippus, it seems, is going to score an important point. For Euthydemus has spoken of silent things, and these he has distinguished from speaking things. He seems, consequently, to have returned to the everyday perspective, where silence and speech limit one another, and all things have limits and bounds.

This, at least, is what Ctesippus imagines, and he points this out to the brothers. But we need to see what he says, and also what *Socrates* thinks.

16. *Ctesippus's Objection*

> But tell me, then, said Ctesippus, are not all things silent?
>
> I presume not, said Euthydemus.
>
> But then, my friend, do all things speak?
>
> Yes, I suppose so—at least those that speak.
>
> But that is not what I asked, said Ctesippus. I asked if all things are silent or speak.
>
> Neither and both! said Dionysodorus, who here rushed in unexpectedly.
>
> At that Ctesippus laughed...Euthydemus, he said, your brother has just put a "both" into your argument. You are worsted and done for now.
>
> And Cleinias, too, was delighted and burst out laughing, and Ctesippus felt that his strength was the strength of ten men. But I personally think that Ctesippus—who is really rather a rogue—overheard these words from the two men themselves; for in no other person living in our time could wisdom like theirs still be found. (300c–e)

Ctesippus thinks he has outwitted the brothers, and yet Socrates denies that this has really happened.[37] Ctesippus, in fact, stole his objection from the brothers—for the brothers cannot be outwitted; they are the wisest men of the day (300e).

---

37. "The young man (Cleinias)," writes Monique Canto, "by bursting into laughter, salutes the victory of Ctesippus, his lover...In effect, the two broth-

Certainly Socrates is right; the brothers have not been outwitted. For when Dionysodorus, responding to Ctesippus's question, says that all things both are and are not silent, and do and do not speak, he does not mean in the least that some things are silent and other things speak. He means, precisely, that all things are silent, and all things speak—and at one and the same time.[38]

Now when does it come about that all things—all material things in the world—rise to the highest level of noise and yet grow profoundly silent? The answer to the question is—Dionysian mystical experience.

We know that Dionysian experience was in many ways an acoustical experience. The coming of the Bacchae meant fantastic amounts of noise, and certain names of Dionysus referred to this noise. He was *bromios* ("clamor king") and *iachus* ("shouter"). But here is a curious fact. It seems that Dionysus was also connected with silence. Euripides calls him *esuchos* ("the quiet one") and uses this word to describe him more than half a dozen times.[39] The Maenads, too—the nurses and consorts of the god—were known for eerie calm and preternatural silence.

Putting all this together, Otto has suggested that the Bacchae experienced "the common root" or "point of identity" between silence and sound or stillness and agitation.[40] If that is so, there must have been a moment in Dionysian experience that conformed to the formula presented by Dionysodorus. The moment must have arrived when the world spoke and yet did not, when the world was silent and yet not, when the most overwhelming sound somehow merged with silence, and the distinction between sound and silence at that point ceased to apply.

---

ers seem to be reduced to silence, as is usual in the vanquished in scenes of eristic battle" (*L'Intrique philosophique*, 186). Canto's view is the prevailing one, but Socrates does not share it.

38. Thus, for the second time, Dionysodorus shows remarkable depth and agility just when we (and Euthydemus) think he is gone wrong.

39. In *The Bacchae*.

40. Walter F. Otto, *Dionysus: Myth and Cult*, trans. Robert B. Palmer (Dallas: Spring Publications, 1981), *passim*.

So we approach the height of mystical ecstasy where silence and sound (or being and non-being) at last prove to be one. It is here that Cleinias rises as if from the dead, giddy with strength-giving laughter. And it is here that Ctesippus, hearing Cleinias's laughter, is filled with the strength of ten men (300d).[41] Moreover, it is here, at this scene of giddy resurrection, that the realm of Platonic ideas comes into view for the first time.

17. *The Ideas*

> Have you, Socrates, asked Dionysodorus, ever yet seen a beautiful thing?
>
> I have, I replied, and many of them.
>
> And did you find them, my dear sir, to be different from the beautiful? Or did you find them, on the contrary, to be the same as the beautiful?
>
> Here, I confess, I felt baffled; and it seemed to me that my bafflement was just compensation for my carping. I replied, however, that though beautiful things were different from the beautiful itself, yet each had some beauty present with it.
>
> In that case, he said, if an ox should happen to be present with you, you would be—an ox. And since I myself am present with you now, you are—Dionysodorus.
>
> Speak decently, I said.
>
> But how can it happen, Socrates, he said, that when a differ-

---

41. Chance writes as follows: "Plato has left no doubt as to the stages of [Ctesippus's] conversion:...from *righteous indignation* at falsehood to a *general acceptance* of the rules of the game, and finally to a warm embrace of the very spirit of eristic itself...We can, I think, safely conclude that Plato has used Ctesippus as a dramatic symbol to illustrate how eristic discourse intoxicated Athenian youth, who then delighted like puppies in pulling about and tearing with words all who approached them. In the bittersweet *aristeia* of this aggressive young man, already given to hubris before his encounter with eristic, we confront that disturbing, disconcerting element which bestows upon the *Euthydemus* the seriousness of tragedy. Through the role of Ctesippus, Plato has granted us privileged access into how this foreign wisdom assisted the other manifestations of sophistry in demoralizing the sons of the marathon-fighters, a privilege we might not have had" (*Plato's Euthydemus*, 174–75).

ent thing is present with a different thing, the different thing is different?

Ah, does that bother you? I asked. Already I was trying to imitate the wisdom of these men, so eager was I to acquire it.

How can I help being bothered, he answered, either I or anyone else, in the face of what cannot be?

What's that you say, Dionysodorus? Is not the beautiful beautiful, and is not the ugly ugly?

Yes, if it seems so to me, he replied.

Then does it seem so?

Certainly, he said.

And the same is the same, and the different different? For I do not suppose that the different is the same, but I would have thought, my friend, that even a child would understand, that the different, indeed, is different. And it seems to me, my dear Dionysodorus, that you have intentionally passed over this one particular point—although, on the whole, I feel that, like craftsmen who are polishing each his special piece of work, you are carrying forward splendidly. (300e–301c)

The realm of ideas at last comes before us—in particular, the idea of beauty. The discussion begins with a question.

Dionysodorus asks Socrates whether he has ever seen anything beautiful, and Socrates replies that he has seen many beautiful things. "In that case," asks Dionysodorus, "were they different from the beautiful, or the same as the beautiful?" And Socrates does not know what to say.[42]

Let us suppose that Socrates replies that beautiful things are different from the beautiful. It will then be pointed out that what is different from the beautiful is not beautiful, and things that are not beautiful are, of course, not beautiful things.

---

42. On the relation between the argument of Dionysodorus (with its Eliatic emphasis) and the Platonic idea of beauty, see Friedländer, *Plato*, 192ff., Sprague; *Plato's Use of Fallacy*, 25; Hawtrey, *Commentary*, 174.

But suppose Socrates replies that beautiful things are the same as the beautiful. It will then be pointed out that if beautiful things are the same as the beautiful, they are also the same as each other, each being simply—the beautiful. There are, consequently, no distinct beautiful things; there is only beauty as such.

Now the first reply—beautiful things are different from the beautiful—deprives things of the beauty that we ordinarily find in them. But the second reply—beautiful things are the same as the beautiful—deprives us of our lives as we ordinarily live them, making everything dissolve into "the great sea of beauty," if we may use this phrase from the *Symposium* (210d). And the brothers are saying that, whoever grumbles against ecstasy, whoever clings so ardently to his unillustrious life that he turns aside in dread when the "sea of beauty" beckons, whoever, in short, resists the state of mind evoked by lovers, mystics, poets, prophets, etc.—will find himself one day in a world with no beauty whatever, the prosaic world of utility that Socrates describes and wants to flee. So what should Socrates reply? Are beautiful things different from "the beautiful," or are they in fact the same?

"I replied," Socrates tells us, "that though beautiful things were different from the beautiful itself, yet each had some beauty present with it." What is the force of this reply?

Let us note, first of all, that the apparently abstract formula "beautiful things are different from the beautiful" describes a perfectly familiar experience. It describes the all-pervasive tone of virtually everyone's everyday life. For, on the one hand, beauty surrounds us everywhere; the world, as a whole, is not only useful but satisfying. And yet the world is different from its beauty. It "stands out" against the background of its beauty, the way stars stand out against the night.

For example, this tree that I can see from the window in the room where I am working—this tangled, leafy mass set against the sky—certainly seems to me beautiful. But where, precisely, is "the beauty?" In what part of the tree is "the beauty?" To the degree that the leaves are leaves, they will not be "the beauty." They will be, precisely, leaves—factories for photosynthesis. And to the degree that the bark is bark, it will not be "the beauty." It will be bark—a thick, unsupple skin. The leaves and the bark and all the other aspects of the tree stand out against "the beauty" and even distract us from "the beauty." So these aspects are different from "the beauty"—yet beauty is unquestionably there.

We may say, then, that the formula used by Socrates exactly applies to the experience of the tree. The tree is a beautiful thing—"it has some beauty present with it"—but the tree is not itself "beauty." It is different from beauty as such.

But perhaps this reply, though it seems to describe our everyday experience, is itself somewhat obscure. For how can the presence of beauty make what is different from beauty beautiful? How can anyone grasp this astonishing transformation?

To indicate the strangeness of it, Dionysodorus considers a parallel case—a case involving Socrates himself. Socrates, let us say, might have been an ox. Those eyes, that nose, those lips, might have been those of an ox. But if Socrates is not an ox, then the presence of an ox will not turn him into an ox. Even in the presence of an ox, Socrates remains a man.

Or again Socrates might have been Dionysodorus. Those eyes, that nose, those lips, might have belonged to Dionysodorus. But if Socrates is not Dionysodorus, the presence of Dionysodorus won't make him Dionysodorus. Even in the presence of Dionysodorus, Socrates remains the man he is.

Now, consider a beautiful thing—let us say, a tree. Those leaves, that bark, that peculiar asymmetrical shape—they might have been "the beautiful." But if the tree is different from "the beautiful," the presence of "the beautiful" (whatever that might mean) will not make the tree beautiful, anymore than the presence of an ox will make Socrates into an ox, or the presence of Dionysodorus will make Socrates Dionysodorus.

At this point, however, something odd seems to happen. The presence of Dionysodorus does, in a way, make Socrates Dionysodorus. For Socrates starts to talk like Dionysodorus. For "already I was starting to imititate the wisdom of these men, so eager was I to acquire it" (301*b*).[43]

And what does Socrates say, now that he is speaking like the brothers? He offers a series of tautologies which are somewhat in the brothers' style. He observes that beauty is beautiful and ugliness is ugly. Further, he observes that the same is the same, and the different is the different. "Even a child," he says, "would understand that the different is...different." And then he stares at the brothers with his deep "bull eyes" and lets them understand that, though he has, indeed, absorbed much of their spirit, and though he is, perhaps, somewhat giddy with their giddiness, he still continues to cherish, and will always cherish, a certain observation with which they seem to disagree—that the different, indeed, is different. "You have," he says, "intentionally passed over this one particular point—although, on the whole...you are carrying forward splendidly" (301*c*).

What can be the meaning of Socrates's response to the brothers? Why does the statement "the different is the different" solve the question concerning beauty and its relation to beautiful things?

Many explanations are possible, but none, I think is certain. Plato intends to be obscure in this passage, and we shall let the obscurity stand, as we have in several other cases. But this much, in any case, is clear. The phrase "the great sea of beauty" which we used a moment ago, having taken it from the *Symposium*, is a phrase that the brothers would have liked, and a phrase that Plato used gladly. In the *Symposium* we read that whoever has fallen in love, and desires to obtain the aim of love, must swiftly renounce the person whom he loves, and open his desire to "the great sea of beauty"—the beauty contained in all beings (210*a*). There is, then, a principle of boundlessness—the brothers' own principle—in all

---

43. Concerning Dionysodorus's discourse about beautiful things and beauty, Hawtrey comments that it is "certain ... that Dionysodorus is using the terminology that we are more accustomed to hearing from the mouth of the Platonic Socrates" (*Commentary*, 175). This is so, and it is striking that here, when the brothers most resemble the Platonic figure of Socrates, that Socrates himself feels an overwhelming impulse to imitate them (301*b*).

transcendence toward ideas. In order to grasp an idea, one must renounce the limits of this or that individual and strive to embrace the "great sea." As a result there will be more than a little of the brothers in the "young and beautiful" Socrates—the Socrates who teaches ideas.

Yet even the radiant Socrates of the middle-period dialogues will cling to the precept that Socrates here sets forth—that the different, indeed, is different. Thus, he will see in beautiful things the boundless absolute beauty, but he will also see difference, and each beautiful thing will stand out from the boundless beauty as the particular thing that it is. In the same way, every trace of wisdom will exhibit boundless wisdom but stand out from boundless wisdom, and every good thing will exhibit boundless goodness, but stand out from boundless goodness—and so on in all other cases.[44] Socrates, then, when he has "gone to school with the brothers" will come to know intimately the great sea of beauty—and of wisdom, goodness, and truth. Yet he never seems to lose himself. He know that "the different is different."

Perhaps there was a time when Socrates almost lost himself—and perhaps Plato hints at this in the remaining part of our text. For though it is true that, when the brothers speak of boundless beauty, Socrates affirms that "the different, indeed, is different," it is also true that the brothers now become more intense and strive toward the darkness of the climax of their presentation. Although Socrates, to be sure, continues to resist, still the great and violent sea that the brothers now unleash crashes down and carries him away.

What, then, will Socrates discover? He will discover pure self-sacrifice. For where Socrates is going—to the realm beyond ideas—all things melt as in a fire, and a spirit of sacrifice prevails. But who is to be sacrificed and how are they to be sacrificed? We will answer these questions below.

---

44. As for the realm of ideas, the same situation prevails. Each idea contains a boundlessness, for each is one, and "oneness" is boundless (*Parmenides*, 137e); but each idea stands out from the others as the specific idea that it is.

18. The Brazier, the Potter, and the Cook

> Do you know, then, he said, what is appropriate for every sort of craftsman? For whom, first of all, is forging brass appropriate?
>
> For the brazier, I said.
>
> And what about making pots?
>
> The potter, I said.
>
> And what about slaughtering and skinning, and cutting the meat into little bits and pieces, and then boiling and roasting.
>
> I could only say: the cook.
>
> Now whoever does the appropriate thing may be said, may he not, to do well?
>
> Yes.
>
> And did you say, Socrates, that cutting and skinning are appropriate for the cook?
>
> I did, but pray forgive me.
>
> Why then, if you slaughter the cook and cut him into bits, and boil and roast him, you will be doing what is appropriate for him, and if you hammer the forger and make the potter into a pot, you will be doing their business likewise. (301c–d)

Our task is to understand why, beyond the realm of ideas, we encounter the sacrifice of—a brazier, a potter, and a cook.

Let us note, first of all, that the brazier, the potter, and the cook, are all going to be burned, and each in his own special fire. The forge has been prepared for the brazier, the kiln for the potter, the hearth for the cook. And who is supposed to sacrifice the brazier, the potter, and the cook? Someone ought to sacrifice them; to do so is his "proper business." But this "someone" seems to be intimately related to the victims of the sacrifice themselves.

Here, as often before, everything depends on syntactical ambiguity. In the Greek sentence, *prosekei...ton mageiron katakoptein kai ekderein*, the noun "the cook" is placed in the accusative, but it could function either as the subject or the object of the infinitive verbs "to cut" and "to skin." Thus, "it is appropriate for the cook to cut and skin" could also be translated as "it is appropriate to cut and skin the cook." Syntactically speaking, then, we are placed in a situation where we seem to see a cook going about his "proper business"—cutting, skinning, roasting, boiling, and so on, but then, when we look again, we discern that Greek syntax has caused a certain reversal. The victim of the cook's "proper business" is now—the cook himself; the cook is the object, not the agent, of this business. So the brazier is forged, and the potter made into a pot, in exactly the same way. What, then, is actually happening?

Obviously, this situation, in which, through a kind of vagueness—in a moment of eerie confusion—someone is caused to discover that he has in some way caused his own ruin—obviously this situation belongs to the sphere of tragedy. For the greatest heroes of tragedy (as Aristotle tells us) undergo a certain "reversal"—which is to say that, through an "error," they perish in chains of events of which they themselves are the cause. There is in the greatest tragedies the "syntactical ambiguity" of which the brothers here make use—and just as the cook cooks himself, and the brazier forges himself, so, too, Oedipus, having brilliantly solved a crime which he himself, long ago, had unknowingly committed, exacts from himself the penalty of enduring life without sight.

But why should tragic self-sacrifice appear in our dialogue beyond the realm of ideas? The answer is that, whoever transcends the ideas enters a sphere where differences are extinguished, and in that sense finds himself sacrificed. But he has risen to this himself, and so he has sacrificed himself, and his death is a tragic death, for his death is victory and transcendence.

But the question still remains as to why our tragic heros are a brazier, a potter, and a cook. Why are these particular figures doomed to tragic self-sacrifice? These figures, let us note first, are all "masters of fire." The fires in which they are immolated are the fires which they themselves kindle, the fires of civilization—the forge, the kiln, and the hearth. These figures, moreover, symbolize human progress. The brazier inaugurates the bronze age, the potter appears at the start of the neolithic, and behind them all stands the cook. It is certainly the cook—the first master of fire—who institutes the *techne* (the art or technology) on which our "human" way of life depends.

So the brothers seem to be speaking to Socrates, who has expressed much concern about the ultimate aim of technology (292c). *Techne* comes to be at the moment described by Cleinias—or was it rather Ctesippus? or a nameless "superior power?"—the moment when a hunter hands over his prey to a cook. Before that, there was no difference between the kill and the feast that followed. But after there was a difference, and soon, many such differences. Technology, Socrates teaches, consists in this system of differences in which every art depends on the art that completes it, as the hunter depends on the cook. But there is no master art—no ultimate "royal" art—to give worth to the system as a whole (292e).

But if Socrates is perplexed because he cannot find the aim of technology (292c), perhaps the solution is to plunge beneath technology. Thus the brazier jumps into the fire, and we renounce the achievements of the bronze age. The potter jumps in the fire, and we renounce the techniques of the new stone age. The cook jumps into the fire, and we renounce the last trace of human art or technology. At last we encounter a hunter who has no need of a cook.

Socrates, we recall, was hoping to find an art which combined production and use (289b). The brothers claimed they could procure one (293b), and this art, precisely, is the art of the primal hunter; the hunter who "uses" his prey as he subdues it, and who does not require a cook to determine the worth of what he gains.

Moreover, we know that Dionysus, god of ecstasy, represents this primal hunter, for he is called *Dionysus Zagreus*, Dionysus the Great Hunter. Since Dionysus Zagreus "delights to eat raw flesh" (as

Euripides, for example, tells us[45]), the Bacchae, in their madness at the height of their ecstasy—set upon live beasts and ate the still living flesh—and so were at one with their god.

What then, awaits us beyond the realm of ideas? There is, to be sure, self-sacrifice, for transcendence requires self-sacrifice. But what is sacrificed is the fire of culture within us, a fire by which we are separated from a much vaster fire—from Dionysus the Great Hunter. Still we have not reached the end.

19. *The Last Sacrifice*

> Gentlemen, I said, you give the finishing touch to your wisdom. But do you think, my friends, that such wisdom will ever come to me? Will it ever be my very own?
>
> Would you recognize it, Socrates, asked Dionysodorus if it did come to be your very own?
>
> If you wanted me to, I would, I said. That much at least is clear to me.
>
> Well, then, Socrates, do you generally know how to tell when things are yours?
>
> I think I do—unless you tell me I don't. For I have my beginning in you, Dionysodorus, and my completion here in Euthydemus.
>
> Then, Socrates, answer this: do you consider things to be "yours" when you are the master of them and can use them just as you please? If we were speaking, for example, of oxen and sheep—would you consider those to be yours which you could sell or bestow as you please, or sacrifice to any god you please? And what you can't treat so, isn't yours?
>
> Now I knew that something brilliant was sure to bob up from these questions; at the same time, I wanted to hear it

---

45. Euripides, *The Bacchae*, 135–40. On the role of *homophagia* (the eating of raw flesh) in Dionysiac religiosity, see Marcel Detienne, *Dionysos Slain*, trans. Mireille and Leonard Muellner (Baltimore: The Johns Hopkins University Press, 1979).

as quickly as possible. I therefore said: of course, that is so. What are mine are things of that sort.

And now, what about this? he asked. Anything that is animate, we are accustomed to call an animal?

Yes.

And you have admitted, have you not, that an animal is yours, when and only when, you can do to it the things I spoke of a moment ago?

Yes, I said.

Now when I made this last concession, Dionysodorus paused for a moment: he paused with an air that seemed almost self-effacing as if he were pondering a matter of ultimate concern. Then he said: Tell me Socrates, have you an ancestral Zeus?

And I, for my part, suspecting the discussion was approaching the place where it ended, tried to escape with a rather desperate dodge, and twisted in the net in which I now knew myself to be taken. My answer was: I have not Dionysodorus.

Why then, what a wretch you are, Socrates, he said, and no Athenian at all! You have no ancestral gods, no sacred rites— it seems you have nothing good or beautiful.

Let me alone, Dionysodorus, I said. Speak decently, I beg you, and do not abuse your pupil. I, too, I assure you, have altars and rites, domestic and ancestral, and everything else that other Athenians have.

Then have not other Athenians their own ancestral Zeus?

None of the Ionians, I said, give him that title—neither those who have settled abroad, nor those living here in our city. We have an ancestral Apollo, because of Ion's parentage. Among us the name "ancestral" is not given to Zeus, but that of "houseward" and "tribal"; and we have a tribal Athena.

That will do, said Dionysodorus. You have, it seems, gods— Apollo and Zeus and Athena.

Certainly, I said.

Then I take it the gods are—yours.

My ancestors, I said, and lords.

In that case, they are yours—or have you still not confessed that this is so?

I have, I said; what else could I do?

And the gods, I presume, are animals. For you have admitted, have you not, that whatever is animate is animal. Or are the gods deprived of life?

They have life.

And when an animal is yours, you may sell it, or bestow it, or sacrifice it to any god you please?

That is so. There is no escape for me, Euthydemus.

Come, then, and tell me: since, as you agree, Zeus and the other gods are yours, is it not the case, Socrates, that you can sell them, bestow them, and treat them just as you please...just like your other animals?

Well, the argument, Crito, knocked me out, so to say, and I lay in a state of speechlessness. Ctesippus, however, came to my rescue—Bravo Hercules! he cried; what a speech! (301e–303a)

There was a feeling among many Greeks, expressed in particular by Aeschylus, that the reign of human technology—of the brazier, the potter, and the cook—began, more or less, with the victory of Zeus over Cronos. In the reign of Cronos, says Aeschylus—and Plato confirms this—people were different from what they are now, for they could "foresee their doom." That is they could "feel" or "see" their death as it approached them with a clarity inaccessible to us now, but which beasts still seem to retain. Possibly that was a golden age, as Hesiod seems to believe, but perhaps, as Aeschylus has it, it was a dark and primitive time where humans lived in caves and resembled beasts in many ways.[46] For

---

46. See David Grene's introduction to *Prometheus Bound* in *The Complete Greek Tragedies*, ed. David Grene and Richmond Lattimore (Chicago: University of Chicago Press, 1956).

Aeschylus, then, humans in the reign of Cronos were entirely without technology, for they had not become masters of fire, and there can be no *techne* without fire.

But when Zeus defeated Cronos, and the Olympian gods took power, the Titan Prometheus—in defiance of Zeus's will—brought fire to humanity. The fire of the hearth became the fire of civilization—of the kiln and the forge, of the potter and the brazier, and so on through many innovations. So, to repeat, the reign of technology coincides with the reign of Zeus. But the experience offered by the brothers carries us to a time anterior to technology, the time of the primal hunter, and therefore to a time when the Olympian gods do not exist or at least have not yet come to power.

Therefore the gods must be dethroned. In truth, the gods must be sacrificed. Yet before being sacrificed, the gods will appear as beasts and thus share in the movement of total regression which the brothers disclose in their speech.

The "argument" here is simple. The gods are "ours" and what is "ours" we can treat as we like (302*a*). Further, the gods are animate, and beings that are animate are animals (302*b*). Therefore the gods are animals with whom we can do what we like. We can buy them, bestow them, sacrifice them, etc. (303*a*).

But what is meant by the striking phrase that appears in the brothers' argument—that then we may sacrifice the gods "to any god we choose" (303*a*)? To what divine being are the gods themselves to be sacrificed, as we journey with the brothers beyond the brazier, the potter, and the cook, to the time of the primal hunter's ecstasy?

The answer to the question is not Dionysus. A return to the time before Zeus and the reign of technology assuredly does not mean a return to Dionysus, for Dionysus, as everyone knows, was actually younger than Zeus. Dionysus was Zeus's child. Dionysus represents the primal hunter—but he is the primal hunter as he persists in the reign of technology; the primal hunter "out of season," if such an expression is not too absurd.

So, once again, to what divine beings are the gods of Olympus to be sacrificed? Before the rise of the Olympians came the age of Cronos and Rhea, and the gods of Olympus themselves flow from

Cronos and Rhea. Still the divisions that haunt human life remain latent with Cronos and Rhea, for this was the time when humans were like gods or beasts, when the sky was closer to earth than it is now, and the cosmos closer to unity.

So perhaps the gods of Olympus, when they take on the form of beasts, are in reality to be sacrificed to the beings from whom they flow—that is, to Cronos and Rhea. Or perhaps, beyond Cronos and Rhea, to the truly primordial figures of whom we read, for example, in Hesiod's *Theogony*—Chaos, Gaia, Erebus, Love, Night.

Now, one further observation. The tragic motif that occurred in our last section occurs again here. But here it is Socrates who plays the tragic hero.

Let us note the peculiar mood of Socrates. He addresses the brothers as if he we speaking to gods, saying, "I have my beginning in you, Dionysodorus, and my completion here in Euthydemus" (301e)—which is precisely a form of address to be found in hymns and prayers.[47] Let us note that Socrates, when he sees where the brothers are leading, "knew that something brilliant was sure to bob up" and "wanted to hear it as quickly as possible" (302a). Perhaps he only means he wanted it over as quickly as possible, but he actually says he wanted "it" as quickly as possible—as if, when he saw "it" coming, he found he keenly desired "it," and wanted "it" quickly achieved.

All this we can set aside. But note that, a moment before the holocaust, Socrates recovers himself and decides to resist as best he can:

> And I, for my part, suspecting the discussion was approaching the place where it ended, tried to escape with a rather desperate dodge, and twisted in the net in which I now felt myself to be taken. (302c)

Why does Socrates speak of a net? Is it not because the net—at least since the *Oresteia* of Aeschylus—has been a prominent symbol of the tragic? Certainly, in tragedy, the hero is caught in a net. But what particular net has caught Socrates?

---

47. See Gifford's commentary for instances in *The Euthydemus of Plato*.

The net is designed as follows. Socrates has admitted that what is "his" he can treat as he likes—sell or bestow or sacrifice to any god he likes. He has also admitted that what is animate is an "animal." Now he is asked if he has an ancestral Zeus. He knows that, as soon as he answers "yes," Zeus will be changed into an animal which is "his" and die like a beast before his eyes.

What, then, should Socrates say? Has he an ancestral Zeus? If he answers "yes," then Zeus dies like a beast. If he answers "no"—if he denies "having" the god—he will seem to have confessed to atheism. This, then, is the tragic net in which Socrates is caught: on the one hand, the sacrifice, the death of the gods in the holocaust; on the other hand, atheism, which denies that the gods live.

The choice is a tragic choice. There is no way out of the net. The question is repeated as Socrates hesitates. Has he an ancestral Zeus? "My answer was: I have not, Dionysodorus."

So it seems the choice is made. The gods are denied, the sacrifice prevented. We know, moreover, the charge for which Socrates was executed—that of denying the gods of the state. Thus Socrates's own sacrifice rises horribly before the mind.

But no, that was a mistake. There has been a misunderstanding. Socrates, it seems, did not really mean it when he denied "having" Zeus. He only meant to deny having "ancestral" Zeus. Now, to deny "ancestral" Zeus is not to deny Zeus. It is an entirely different matter.

Now the room is quiet and light pours in as from a dream. Socrates steps back, and slowly he speaks:

> None of the Ionians, I said, give him that title—neither those who have settled abroad nor those living here in our city. We have an ancestral Apollo, because of Ion's parentage. Among us the name "ancestral" is not given to Zeus, but that of "houseward" and "tribal" and we have a tribal Athena.
>
> That will do, said Dionysodorus. (302*d*)

So, once again, the Olympians come before us—radiant, wise, and in all ways perfectly formed. Then, as must happen—and as the brothers had foretold—the Olympians turn into beasts and die into vaster divinities. "Bravo Hercules!" yells Ctesippus, delighted with the argument. But Socrates is silent, lying speechless as if from a blow (303*a*).

And here, my dear Crito, everyone who was present—everyone, I say, without exception—wildly extolled the argument and the two men; and all nearly died of laughing, clapping and rejoicing. Of course, the brothers had been applauded every time they scored a point; but the applause, until now, had come only from their pupils. But now, Crito, if I may put it in this fashion, the very pillars of the Lyceum betook themselves to clapping and joined in the joy and acclaim. (303*b*)

What is unknown can become known, but what is unknowable remains fundamentally and always unable to be known; and it is precisely this psychic unconsciousness, beyond the reach of insight and knowledge, that the anima mediates. She makes us unconscious. As she is the very craziness of life, she drives us crazy... The deeper we follow her, the more fantastic consciousness becomes.

    JAMES HILLMAN, *Anima: An Anatomy of a Personified Notion*

Recognizing the shadow is what I call the apprenticeship, but making out with the anima is the masterpiece which not many can bring off.

    C. G. JUNG, *Letter to Traugott Egloff,* 9 February 1959

CHAPTER EIGHT

Conclusion

1. *Socrates's Praise of the Brothers*

For my part, Crito, I was quite disposed to admit that I had never encountered anyone as wise as these two men. I was in fact quite enslaved by their wisdom; and I turned to the singing of its praise. This is what I said: O happy pair! What amazing genius to have brought to perfection so quickly so great an achievement as this! For there are many excellent features, Euthydemus and Dionysodorus, encompassed in your discourse. And among these, you know, I would say the most magnificent is that you care not a jot for what the masses think, nor solemn-seeming men of great reputation, but only for people like yourselves. For I know very well that there are few men like you who appreciate arguments like yours; the rest, I assure you, would feel more ashamed to refute their opponents with your methods, than to be refuted by them. I also detect in your work a certain gentle democratic feature to which I desire to call attention. For when you tell us there is nothing either beautiful, or good, or white, or anything else, and that, quite generally, nothing differs from anything, you not only stitch up the mouths of all other people, which is what you say you do, but you stitch up your own mouths as well, and this very courteous gesture takes all offense from your words. Best of all, you have contrived your method so artfully and shrewdly that absolutely anyone can learn it in a trice—I myself, you know, observed our Ctesippus here, and I saw how quickly he learned on the spot to imitate you. Now insofar as your achievement can be imparted very quickly, it is a fine thing; on the other hand, for large numbers of hearers, I do not think it is suitable; and if you take my advice, you will avoid speaking to crowds, lest everyone master your routine in a short time, and then forget to thank you for your pains. But the best thing for the two of you, I think, would be simply to speak exclusively with each other—or if a third person is present, let him at least pay a fee. And I think, if you are prudent, you will share this advice with your pupils—that they should never speak to anyone except you and each other. For it is the rare, Euthydemus, that is precious, while water, though cheapest, is best, as Pindar says. But come, I said, and see if you can admit young Cleinias and me to your class. (303*c*–304*b*)

In these ironic parting words, Socrates makes it clear that Euthydemus and Dionsydorus are different from other people, and, so to speak, in a class by themselves; and yet, in another way, they are the same as other people—are in fact superbly "democratic."

The brothers, first of all, are different from other people because they care not a jot for what other people think, not even the wisest people; and because their way of speaking is so far beyond the normal that no one else could endure using it, no matter how potent it seemed. The brothers, we may say, are either gods or beasts; and we may place them at the top—or else, perhaps, at the bottom—of a hierarchically organized humanity.

On the other hand, the brothers are also the same as other people, because the power they embody is latent in us all, and anyone—e.g., Ctesippus—can quite easily learn to imitate them; then, too, the brothers are the same as other people, because they themselves deny the reality of difference, and say that nothing is beautiful or good, or white or black, and so on. Further, the brothers are the same as other people because when, by means of their arguments, they "stitch up" everyone's "mouth," they also, simultaneously, stitch up their own mouths; and because they include themselves in the great conflagration they cause, they show that their violence is the best sort of violence—the gentle democratic sort (303*d*).

We can see, in short—to sum up Socrates's praise—that though the brothers—being gods and beasts, are at the top and at the bottom of the whole human hierarchy, they also represent the denial of all hierarchy—the collapse of all distinctions in the measureless.

And with this we arrive at the last words uttered by Socrates, as he takes his leave of Euthydemus and Dionysodorus. These last words are important, and we need to read them again.

> But the best thing for the two of you, I think, would be simply to speak exclusively with each other—or if a third person is present, let him at least pay a fee...For it is the rare, Euthydemus, that is precious, while water, though cheapest, is best, as Pindar says. But come, I said, and see if you can admit young Cleinias and me to your class. (304*b*)

The brothers, Socrates says, should suppress or conceal their "gentle democratic" leveling, on pain of being held "cheap"—they should, in other words, express the principle of hierarchy and appear in the guise of gods and beasts. But are there gods and beasts? And is there really a hierarchy? Possibly Socrates has doubts. Hence his very last words.

It is the rare, Socrates says, that stands at the top of the hierarchy, and the reason, of course, is that the rare is held to be precious. But the rare, though it is precious, is yet not the best; for—"water is best, as Pindar said" (304*b*).

And having thus conceded the point that, finally, "water is best," Socrates requests that he be permitted to join the brothers' class. But *why* is water best? What does it mean to say "water is best?" We shall answer these questions below.

2. *Water and Gold*

> Best of all things is water, but gold, like a gleaming fire,
> By night outshines all pride of wealth beside.

These are the opening lines of Pindar's first Olympic ode, which Socrates cites to the brothers. The lines speak of gold; and the *Euthydemus*, too, speaks of gold in several places (289*a*, 298*a*, 299*e*). But the lines speak also of water, and say that water is best. Once again, then, what does this mean?

Certainly, Pindar's lines may be interpreted in many ways. Pindar himself intended this multiplicity. But we will limit ourselves to one interpretation; the most pertinent to our task. "Water," says Pindar, "is best." Why is it that "water is best?"

Let us note that there is a feeling, expressed in a universal symbolism, that water is *materia prima:* all things rise out of water; all return, at their destruction, to water; and what seems to be other than water is still made out of water: it is water in a special form or state. Now this spontaneous intuition about the omnipresence of water—which modern science, as we know, finds somewhat close to the truth—was taken up by Thales, the first of the Greek philosophers. "The source of all things," says Thales, "is water."

And now, let us consider that if water is the source, what does it mean to say "water is best?" It means that the source is best, that *materia prima* is best; that all things emerge and are made from the best. It means, too, that wherever we happen to be—or whatever we work with or see or encounter—we do not, for a moment, depart from that which is best: the best is simply—inescapable. And yet, even though "water is best" (so that everything, finally, is best), even so, Pindar writes, "...gold, like a gleaming fire,/by night outshines all pride of wealth beside" (*Olympia,* 1.1–2).

Now just as there is a universal symbolism attached to water, so there is a universal symbolism attached to gold. Gold is associated with fire, with the sun, with light, wisdom, truth; in a view recorded by Plato, gold is *to kalon,* the essence of beauty and nobility (*Hippias Major,* 289e). There is a feeling, moreover, which provides the basis of alchemy, that gold is the fulfillment of matter; gold, in other words, is what all matter would be, if given enough time to "progress." Thus, the source (water) is after all not the best. The source is only the beginning. There are real differences; there is something to strive for and mount toward; there is that which blazes out the way a fire blazes at night—there is, in a word, gold.

Once again, let us read Pindar's lines: "Best of all things is water, but gold, like a gleaming fire,/By night outshines all pride of wealth beside." A world of philosophic wisdom is contained in the lines, in the tension of which they speak. Let us speak of this tension more clearly.

In the first place, water is best, the omnipresent source of things is best. For we can see that, if the best is really best—the best we can conceive—then it is good enough, strong enough, to diffuse its presence everywhere and to saturate all places, which means that the best, boundlessly present, leaves no room for what is not best; the best is simply the real. It is true, to be sure—as Meister Eckhart once confessed—that we normally prefer the sound of beautiful music to the sound of a dripping faucet; the dripping faucet seems less than the best. But it is also true—as Meister Eckhart knew quite well—that if we could really hear the dripping of the faucet, if we could judge it, for once, by its own proper standard and not impose another standard, derived, for example, from music—if, in short, we could really grasp the substance of the sound of the dripping—we would find in it a supreme and limitless good, and so we would find "the best." And this is the brothers' truth. Euythydemus expresses this truth in his *pasi panta homoios* ("all are equally in all"), which Plato cites in the *Cratylus*. For if "all are equally in all," then none can take precedence over any other, and a sharp leveling wind blows through the cosmos. But this wind has never ceased to blow, and our task is simply to discern it. We must peer into things until we find the boundless worth in them (for the whole world's worth dwells in each of them), and we must respond to the boundless worth with a feeling of boundless desire, for boundless worth must elicit boundless need. Therefore, water is best.

Yet, Pindar writes—and the longing of the poet is evident in his lines—"...gold, like a gleaming fire,/by night outshines all pride of wealth beside." It is, perhaps, then, in a somewhat cautious spirit that Pindar admits that "water is best;" for he is certainly drawn to gold, and to the brightness of fire and the sun, and particularly to the victories in great athletic contests which provide the theme of his songs. In the same way, it seems proper and inevitable that we should prefer music to mere dripping water, and justice to injustice, and harmony to discord, and in general that we should subordinate—and subordinate repeatedly—a good to a better and a better to a still better, in the hope of arriving at an ultimate "best"—which means, as Socrates says, that we play the game of *ho dios Korinthos*, setting up and tearing down kings. To be sure, "water is best;" still, gold embodies transcendence. So, we seem to restore the hierarchy which a moment ago had collapsed—but it is sure to collapse again.

Everyone is aware of the "gold standard" in Plato, but it is right to become aware of the "water standard" as well. In the *Cratylus*, for example, Socrates speaks of a doctrine in which all forms are bad and have to be overturned, overturned so that the deep substance of things—what we may call the Heracleitian flux in them—may be released and brought to light.

In the *Thaetetus*, again, Socrates experiments with a metaphysical relativism, in which the whole of human experience is broken into fragments—and each fragment, it seems, may be said to be equally "true", since there is no standard of truth to impose on it from outside.

In the *Parmenides*, again—which is Plato's speculative masterpiece—a hierarchy emerges with "the One" on top and "the Others" at the bottom—but this top and bottom turn out to be the same, so that the top and bottom are (as mystics say) the same, and we have not, consequently, been rising or falling in a hierarchy after all (for the hierarchy fades when the top and bottom prove the same) but have merely been turning in a single luminous point, a point which is being itself.

We could speak, too, of the "great sea of beauty" which emerges in the *Symposium* (210*d*), of the principle of "continuity" which is offered in the *Hippias Major* (300*b*), of the critique of all reflection which is developed in the *Charmides* (167*b*–169*d*), and—most of all—but in a slightly different way—of the mysterious apology on behalf of intoxicated madness (= Dionysus) that is offered in the *Laws*, Books One and Two.

But to pursue all this would serve no purpose in this place. Our point is simply that, just as it would be absurd to suppress the principle of hierarchy in Plato, which Plato assuredly loves, so it would be absurd to suppress the principle of boundlessness in Plato, by which Plato is strangely fascinated. For Plato, like Pindar, knows that water is best, and that gold shines forth extraordinarily.

But to return to the *Euthydemus*, Plato seems to have written this dialogue in a mood of grim humor and with a feeling of anxiety verging, almost, on despair. For here the principle of hierarchy is made to seem particularly fruitless, since we learn, in Hamlet's phrase, that "The King is a Thing of nothing...," but here the principle of boundlessness, which one rightly opposes to the King, is made to seem rather sinister—at times like a very evil dream.

But if our dialogue expresses anxiety, it also expresses hope. For what happens is that Socrates, having abandoned the principle of hierarchy, undertakes with his instructors a leap into the boundless; and he survives this leap, survives this nightmare of regression, and he emerges a new man—a "young and beautiful" man. And this is the man who will present the theory of ideas in the most beautiful dialogues of Plato.

The *Euthydemus*, in short, which expresses a certain despair, also expresses the great initiation by which Plato (and Socrates?) conquered this despair. The theme of initiation leads back to Pindar's ode, for Pindar, too, speaks of a great initiation—that of Pelops, the son of Tantalus. Let us turn once again to Pindar's ode.

3. *The Suffering and Victory of Prince Pelops*

...[Hieron's] fame shines
among strong men where Lydian Pelops went to dwell,
Pelops that he who clips the earth in his great strength,
Poseidon, loved, when Klotho lifted him out
of the clean cauldron, his shoulder gleaming ivory...
Son of Tantalus, against older men I will say
that when your father summoned the gods
to that stateliest feast at beloved Sipylos,
and gave them to eat and received in turn,
then he of the shining trident caught you up,
his heart to desire broken, and with his horses and car of gold
carried you up to the house of Zeus and his wide honor,
where Ganymede at a later time
came for the same desire in Zeus.
But when you were gone, and men from your mother looked,
  nor brought you back,

> some man, a neighbor, spoke quietly for spite,
> how they took you and with a knife
> minced your limbs into bubbling water
> and over the table divided and ate
> flesh of your body...
>
> I cannot understand how any god could gorge thus; I recoil.
> Many a time disaster has come to the speakers of evil.
>
> >   PINDAR, *Olympia*, 1 (trans. Richmond Lattimore)

Here we are going to speak of Pelops—but there are two stories about Pelops. There is a traditional story, which Pindar repeats and rejects, and an "innovative" story, which Pindar himself perhaps invented.

According to the traditional story, Pelops suffers the fate of being murdered by his father, and then dismembered, cooked, and served at table. The guests at the banquet are the Olympian gods. One of them, Demeter, who has arrived at the meal late, actually tastes the dish; the others refrain, but all are angry at what Tantalus has done. But now the gods put the pieces of Pelops into a magic cauldron. The pieces are boiled together, and soon Pelops comes back to life. An ivory shoulder is constructed for him to replace what Demeter had unknowingly eaten. This ivory shoulder will be the permanent mark of his ordeal.

Such, then, is the suffering of Pelops. No doubt, its point is obscure. Tantalus seems to assume that the gods of Olympus are savage and cruel and would welcome human sacrifice, but the gods demonstrate clearly that they are not like that at all—the meal they are given is altogether repulsive to them. But perhaps Tantalus's intention had been all along to deceive the gods, and to force them by his sacrifice to confer some enormous benefit. Pelops, at least, profits greatly from his ordeal. He rises from the cauldron, his ivory shoulder gleaming, no longer a boy but a man.

He proves his manhood as follows: There is a princess, Hippodameia, the most glorious woman of her day. She has not yet married. The reason she has not married is that her father, the evil Oenomaus, is jealous of her beauty and intends to keep her for himself—so when suitors come forward, he challenges them to a chariot race, and kills them during the race, cutting them down with spears. Thirteen suitors have died in this way. Pelops, however, challenges Oenomaus and does not die, but prevails. Then he marries Hippodamaeia and fathers six admirable sons.

Such, then, is the traditional story of Pelops—the story known to Pindar's hearers. Certainly there is glory, but the boiling comes first of all.

Now let us turn to the "revisionist" story of Pelops, the version favored by Pindar. Here, the glory remains, but the boiling is replaced by something different. In fact, Pindar tells us, the story of the boiling of Pelops was only an invention of the jealous neighbors of Pelops. Jealous neighbors whispered:

> how they took you and with a knife
> minced your limbs into bubbling water,
> and over the table divided and ate
> flesh of your body...

but actually none of this happened.

Pelops, to be sure, is transmuted by the gods into a hero, but not in this appalling manner. What actually happens is this: Pelops, it seems, is a very beautiful youth, so beautiful, in fact, that the god Poseidon falls in love with him. Visiting Tantalus at a banquet—a "stately" innocent banquet—Poseidon sees Clotho lift him out "of the clean cauldron, his shoulder gleaming ivory," and at that moment "his heart to desire broke." Certainly, then, there is a cauldron, as all the storytellers tell us, but it is merely a purifying cauldron; no violence precedes its use. Certainly, Pelops has an ivory shoulder, as all the stories report, but far from being a mark of violence, it is a mark of beauty and purity, and it arouses a god's desire.

Poseidon, then, carries Pelops in a chariot of gold up to the house where "Ganymede, in later times, came for the same desire in Zeus." Pelops, let us repeat, is in no way boiled in water but is transported in a chariot of gold—and so the motif of water and gold occurs again in the poem.

Carried off by Poseidon, Pelops vanishes from the world, and for a long time no one encounters him. Thus the neighbors gossip maliciously. Pelops, doubtless, would have stayed with the gods forever, far from time and death—except for his father's sin.

For Tantalus, it seems, is a doomed figure, even in Pindar's innovative version of the story. The gods have given him the elixir of immortality and he has shared it with his friends, without obtaining the gods' consent. It is for this—and nothing else—that he is punished. And since the son of a fallen father cannot remain in the gods' house, Pelops must return to our shifting, transitory world.

"If we must die," he cries gallantly, "why die without glory?" Bodied forth by heaven, he appears as a hero on earth. And since he is no longer a boy, drawn to older males, he decides to undertake the most glorious courtship possible, the courtship of the radiant Hippodameia.

But for this, he requires help. And so alone, in the darkness, he races toward the sea, and loudly he calls upon Poseidon, with whom he had formerly dwelt. The god instantly appears, and pleased by the young man's daring, he offers certain necessary gifts—a chariot made of gold, and unwearying horses with wings. (Note, once again, the juxtaposition of water and gold.)

This, then, is the "innovative" story of Pelops, which Pindar himself may have invented. The new version resembles the old, in that it shows how a youth rises to greatness as a hero. But the youth's initiation is erotic, rather than tragic. He is loved in a realm beyond time, not killed, dismembered, and cooked.

Of course, we do not intend to discuss the complexity of Pindar's poem, which would require, perhaps, a book longer than the one we are concluding. It is clear, however, that the water, which is "best" in the first line of the poem, becomes the water of torment in which the boy Pelops is boiled; and the "gold like a gleaming fire" in the first line of the poem becomes the gold of the magical chariot in which Pelops flies to glory and to love. But the poem remains ambiguous because Poseidon, the giver of gold, cannot be the opposite of water; he is the god of water. And Pelops, finally, as soon as he dreams of Hippodameia, must encounter the god by water—for

Pindar tells us plainly how he rushed through the darkness to the water, and there evoked the god's aid.

Now let us return to Plato. Plato, of course, was a teacher—one of the greatest of teachers. Plato wanted to know how to "improve" the young—how to raise them up to the ideal. Obviously, Plato was a "modern" educator. He taught math, science, politics, rhetoric, and assorted "Socratic" techniques for calling one's life into question—but to him all these were merely means. What most interested Plato was something rather like heroism. He aimed to instill in the young a new power of being, and for this he had to lead them to the power of being as such.

We can see that this is so concerning Plato. His myth of the cave makes this clear to us. The cave, plainly, is "the cave of initiation," where strange games are played and hallucinations induced. The novice is led (or dragged) to new being for he is taken out of the cave and restored to a sphere of light. But the myth of the cave is—a myth. It speaks in symbols only. Yet we would like to know, in a somewhat more literal way, how the sphere of light is obtained.

In fact, there are two different paths. The first path is suffering, the way of the boiling cauldron. To obtain new being, to be open to the power of being, means first of all, to "die" to oneself—to renounce the ego by which one is tightly bound to oneself. Hence all the horrors of tragedy: the boiling, the flaying, and so on. These make the ego dissolve, leaving space for a power beyond.

But the other path is love, love rather than suffering—and first the love beyond time of a god for human reality. Certainly one may conceive of non-tragic initiation, where one is not, so to say, "torn apart" into openness to being, but led by the power of being to open oneself in love.

This "erotic" initiation is what Pindar described in his ode and what he preferred to the boiling. Plato, too, preferred this. He devoted his life to this. Thus Plato shows us Socrates—homely, charismatic Socrates—Socrates who offers an entirely ascetic yet erotic initiation. Alcibiades, in the *Symposium*, speaks of the experience entailed (222c).

Plato, on the other hand, understood the dark or tragic mode of initiation. He describes it in the *Euthydemus*, using all its terrible imagery. And there is a world of meaning in the story—which is, almost certainly, a true story—that Plato, as a youth, desired to write tragedies, but Socrates, his teacher, showed him another path.

AFTERWORD

Politics and Philosophy

The presentation in the Euthydemus *is so vivid that we forget it isn't actually happening, but only being remembered. All the voices in the dialogue—the two brothers, Ctesippus, Cleinias, the noisy listeners—are actually emerging from the singular voice of Socrates, and all for the benefit of Crito, who saw the performance from afar without hearing it. The recollection has now ended, and Socrates and Cleinias continue their conversation:*

Crito: I feel, Socrates, that it's ridiculous for me to admonish you, but I need to tell you something I heard just now. You should know that one of those who left your discussion came up to me when I was pacing—someone who thinks himself clever, and who really does have a gift for turning out speeches for the courts…He came up to me and said: Well, Crito, if you had been there in that crowd just now, you would have been ashamed, I can tell you, for your particular friend Socrates. It was so strange how he consented to lend himself to those men; they just play games with phrases and don't care in the least about the meaning…And my view, Socrates, is that it would be wrong to criticize the practice of philosophy…but it was right to blame engagement with such people, especially before a crowd.

Socrates: Of which party was the man who came up to you…

Crito: Well, he wasn't an orator, and I don't think he's ever in court, but people say he knows a lot about it, and it's really a marvelous thing how he composes such superb speeches.

Socrates: Now I understand. I was just going to speak of such people. They are the ones who stand, as Prodicus says, on the borderline between philosophy and politics. And they think themselves cleverer than anyone, and lots of people agree with them. And maybe their view is reasonable after all, since they regard themselves as having a measured commitment to philosophy and a measured engagement in politics; and so they have a share in both—in each as needed (304c–305e).

My commentary ended at 304c, with Socrates's farewell to the brothers. There were three more pages in the dialogue, which formed a sort of "afterword"; and they corresponded to the introductory pages where Socrates, before reciting the whole performance, notes that the brothers in the past practiced law (where practical matters were at stake); and prior to that, kick-boxing (where combat was purely physical). In brief, their career spans a continuum, from bodily strife to sophistical-mystical enlightenment (271d–272c); and at the end of the dialogue comes a shift in the other direction; for we hear from a "seeker of wisdom" who slides into politics successfully. When (in the 1990s) I worked on this book, I was able to comment briefly on the opening pages of the dialogue, but regarding these last pages I felt a constraint and wrote nothing. I remembered even then, however, that, when I first read the dialogue (still a university student), these last pages impressed me (as indeed they impress me today), and probably they persuaded me to read again more carefully.

What is striking about these final pages? The wild images have faded; the friends are speaking quietly; and a bit of potential awkwardness (honesty having forced Crito to agree with the outsider's criticism) is handled very tactfully, as an occasion for further discussion. And given Socrates's recent quest for a prescient "royal art" of governance, it is right that the question of political activity should be raised once again.

The obtrusive person who speaks ill of Socrates—behind his back, so to say—is someone who believes that a "mere" philosopher, that is, a philosopher detached from matters of the polis, will inevitably decline into the playing of conceptual games, something frivolous, or too narrow, or mad. Socrates's discourteous critic has been taken, at times, to be Isocrates, who considered himself, indeed, to be an authentic philosopher, even as he wrote speeches for the courts and politicians and princes. Isocrates could charge twenty talents for a single speech;[1] and that gave proof of his "seriousness," in contrast to Socrates's frivolity.

Should philosophers lend themselves to politics? Crito's acquaintance thinks so. On the other hand, Socrates's daimon—that numinous presence that infallibly "speaks" when things are wrong, its "silence" implying all is well—bars Socrates's participation in political activity. Yet this prescient daimon would have been a great ally in the political arena, had it not blocked the way so insistently.

Citing the sophist Prodicus, Socrates refers to his critic as a "border" person—as a person standing on the borderline between the philosophic realm and the political. Is that really a desirable location? Are the border people right in thinking that by placing themselves between two regions, they can "have a share of both," and perhaps be more than either singly? Everything depends on whether philosophy and politics ultimately seek the same object. If certain politicians seek the good (as they learn to do in the utopian *Republic*), if they see in the light of the good what choices bring the best outcomes, they will to that extent share the aim of Platonic philosophy and their actions will merge with it seamlessly.

Since writing my commentary, I've thought a lot about leaders of all kinds. Plato asks: can we train our youth to be leaders? If we put together from the *Republic* the "parable of the cave" with its elaboration (all in Book 7), and if we add to it Socrates's death-day "autobiography" where he tells of his career as a young natural scientist (*Phaedo*, 96a–107a), we can detect Plato's curious view of a future leader's education. This is not the place for that, but roughly it is a journey of intensification and expansion. Familiar objects unfold in new dimensions, as if flattened shadows were becoming rounded figures, their vibrant colors emerging; or it is as if every point revealed a line coiled within, and every line a plane, and every plane a solid, and patterns of cosmic motion opened out into ethi-

---

1. Pliny, *Natural History*, 7.30.

cal dimensions, all suspended in the good. Crucially, the program combines ethical conversation, science, and mathematics, and pure meditation on objects as they manifest—it is a program overturning boundaries, so to say. Socrates's afternoon with Euthydemus and Dionysodorus likewise offers expansion and intensification: manic energy, boundaries dissolving, worlds unfolding within worlds.

What is more, the joy of all this unfolding is inevitably tempered by dread—in the classroom of the future leaders, as much as in the brothers' classroom. This is because the good, whether approached through science or philosophical meditation, burns and shines so fiercely that it makes one desperate for security. Socrates knows about this, because, in his early days as a scientist, he first studied science reductively (*Phaedo*, 96a–d), and then, rectifying that, he detected beyond nature's patterns a brightness so overwhelming that he dropped out of science altogether (*Phaedo*, 97b–100b). He called the frightening brightness—optimistically—the good. And if the neophytes destined to be leaders survive their ordeals and, unlike Socrates, "gaze at the sun" unflinchingly (*Republic*, 516b), they will, indeed, have learned to govern wisely. But the people, Socrates warns, will eventually turn against them, unless they share their leaders' enlightenment (*Republic*, 517a). Socrates's own fate is thus foreseen.

Nevertheless, philosophy can influence politics. The border regions exists. Alexander (later called "the Great") studied with Aristotle and conquered the known world; Dionysius, King of Syracuse, brought Plato to his court to be his teacher; and Socrates worked with Alcibiades, his "beloved disciple," as it were. On the other hand, Aristotle's pupil died (or was killed) before he could govern his conquests; and Plato's work with Dionysius was thwarted by recalcitrant forces; and Alcibiades—who had, indeed, an amazing capacity to sense "what needed to be done," as if enjoying, like his teacher, a certain daimonic privilege—is exiled (twice) from his city; for the city was frightened of his gifts and his rebelliousness, and especially of the "impiety" they sensed in him, as they had with his teacher Socrates. The people had the feeling that, if these two had their way, "new divine beings" would replace "the gods the state believed in" (*Apology*, 25b), as if, to cite the ghastly

Euthydemian joke, the gods—if they exist—must be sacrificed to powers beyond them (301e–303b).

This is not the place to tell the story of Alcibiades. But let us note that our dialogue, if it somehow actually happened, would have happened between the death of Alcibiades (which Socrates refers to explicitly) and the death of Socrates himself. During that period, the Athenians were crushed by the Spartans and subjected to a reign of terror. And many Athenians believed that they would not have suffered so brutally if Alcibiades had lived; for he would have known how to save them, since for him the impossible was possible;[2] and the hope of a new Alcibiades would have stirred across the city the maddest expectations—such as reverberate, it seems to me, in the brothers' initiatory practice. (Young Cleinias, who has the Alcibidian radiance and comes from Alcibiades's family, confirms by his presence in the dialogue that we are to think of Alcibiades while reading it. Yet Cleinias seems rather passive: he is mostly a kind of cipher—like a figure in a dream in whom multiple meanings converge but who somehow never becomes vivid. On the other hand, Cleinias does emerge briefly from his silence—at the very center of the dialogue—saying strong words ["...such words from a strippling!"] about transcending the art of speechwriters and generals by grasping a finality they lack (289d–290d). And Alcibiades, to say the least of him, was an excellent general and speechmaker, and combined these gifts in a higher, more numinous capacity—though he may, to point again to a theme of the dialogue, have used his gifts unwisely, tragically [280b–281e].)

Alcibiades at times seemed so capable, however, that people came to believe there was "nothing [he could] not do,"[3] which is exactly what the brothers assert of themselves so ecstatically (293a–296d). Going further: the discourse of Alcibiades was reportedly so hyp-

---

2. Plutarch, *Parallel Lives*, "Alcibiades," 32, 38.

3. Plutarch writes: "Alcibiades seems to be a clear case of someone destroyed by his own reputation. His successes had made his daring and resourcefulness so well known that any failure prompted people to wonder whether he had really tried. They never doubted his ability; if he really tried, they thought, nothing would be impossible for him" (Ibid., 35).

notic that everything that he said felt true because he said it, as if reality had to be what Alcibiades named it—this is the magic language the brothers' keep evoking (283e–287d). Indeed, the image of Alcibiades, his greatness and his atrocities, may itself, a distinguished scholar warns, have its origin in lies that Alcibiades himself told fellow exile Thucydides, the historian who was writing about events as they unfolded.[4] Alcibiades's personality seemed indeed to be all personalities ("all things dwelling in all," says Euthydemus as quoted in the *Cratylus* [386d]); and one could see in Alcibiades whatever, or whomever, one desired.[5] Praising Socrates, Alcibiades notes in the *Symposium* that Socrates possesses a "Corybantic" magnetism, as if the philosopher's rational discourse had the quality of Corybantic music (215d); but more publicly it was Alcibiades whose charisma was so irresistible, and who evoked the adoration that the *Euthydemus* explores. Truly, there was a cult of Alcibiades. Had he not mimicked privately the sacred rites of Eleusis, performing them with friends, even as the brothers mimic the rites of the Corybantes? Alcibiades was tried for profaning the mysteries of Eleusis, but he later became the protector of Eleusis—indeed for a moment he became its high priest and hierophant.[6] Indeed, what he pictured in his mind often became shared reality.

His story is amazing, unbelievable. The most disturbing words in our dialogue, "You desire your darling dead," are spoken about Cleinias, but surely apply to Alcibiades. "They love him, they hate him," writes Aristophanes of Alcibiades (1425). Many of those who were drawn to him also desired his death and could not resolve their ambivalence. Alcibiades himself knew this ambivalence with respect to his teacher Socrates. He revered Socrates but at times desired his death, because Socrates showed him an ideal he couldn't embody, and Socrates implanted in him what he otherwise wouldn't have known: a sense of shame (*Symposium*, 216b–c).

---

4. Donald Kagan, *The Peloponnesian War* (London: Penguin Books, 2003).
5. Plutarch, *Parallel Lives*, 23.
6. Ibid., 34.

AFTERWORD: Politics and Philosophy

Sometime in 1995, I submitted this manuscript to Spring Publications, but without the notes from James Hillman, whose writing, at the time, I hadn't read, and without the page on the daimon (in the preface), about which, at the time—not having read *The Soul's Code*—I did not have very much to say. When Spring Publications accepted the manuscript, I began to read Hillman carefully, and found in Archetypal Psychology an enterprise I believed in, a creative form of Platonism that could evolve beyond the classroom, as people of all kinds supported one another in the Socratic quest for lucidity. From Hillman's books, I copied the most pertinent passages and, with the editor's permission, I added them as endnotes to my commentary. And now, twenty-two years later—with the endnotes turned into footnotes—I find it difficult to believe they weren't guiding the book I was writing. And perhaps they actually were; for we can be influenced, I sometimes think, by books we haven't read but will read, just as ancient texts can respond with enigmatic precision to the distant needs of future readers. According to the rabbis, the revelation at Sinai was shaped by the questions of all who would later encounter it because the speaker, in this case, was not confined to any moment of time. But classics texts are often like that. Don't the gods (who see the future) speak through all great poets, as Socrates says (*Apology*, 22a–d)? And that's why Plato was right against Socrates when he bet on the art of writing. Written words aren't necessarily dead, as if confined to their ink, which was what Socrates feared when he warned students against them (*Phaedrus*, 274c–276c). The best ancient words do seem to know who we are, as if subliminally their author were acquainted with us.

In the past twenty-two years, many themes of this manuscript seem to have echoed frighteningly across the political world: our domination of nature and our distance from it; our failure to sense likely outcomes—existentially—in contrivances of the moment; the question of truth and the magic of words that shape reality; our post-truth political discourse that exhausts critical thinking; cults and cult leaders, both religious and secular, whose images manifest globally on billions of screens; and finally an encompassing plague that requires expiation and renewal. Just before the release of this book in 1999, I completed an essay on Aristophanes's *The Clouds* and submitted it to the *Spring Journal* for its issue on Education, which was scheduled for 2002.[7] In *The Clouds*, Socrates swings back and forth in a basket suspended on a crane—he has detached himself from nature but wields power through sophistry and science. At the end of the play, his high-flying Thinkery is torched. It burns and falls to the ground, a victim of religious terrorism. His former student, hearing divine voices, couldn't stop himself from striking in this way.[8] On September 11, 2001, when the Twin Towers fell, it seemed to me that religious terrorism had in a similar way claimed another icon. And the strike was brought about by a hypnotic cult leader, whose discourse seemed to followers to shape their reality, the very thing about which I had written—had "lent myself" to, perhaps excessively—in the book you now hold in your hands. In *The Clouds*, by which the *Euthydemus* was certainly influenced, Socrates lectures (somewhat incongruously) on finance and trade, as if he were alluding to the World Trade Center, whose heartbreaking fall we were watching that day. Particularly uncanny to me—since I had placed in this book a chapter called "Two, not One"—was the fact that the Towers were twin. They had presided over New York like giant Dioscuri; and when the terrorists struck, everything happened twice: two planes, two towers, one tragedy echoing another, as the brothers echo each other in Cleinias's initiatory "chairing."

Euphemei, says Socrates. Speak reverently. So I would like to end with another image, that of the "young and beautiful" Socrates emerging from Plato's cauldron. Let us read again the lines that Plato wrote to Dionysius, King of Syracuse, who wished to study with him:

> What has been written must be disclosed. That is why there is not, and never can be, any work of Plato's own. What

---

7. Carl Levenson, "Socrates' School," *Spring: A Journal of Archetype and Culture* 69 (2002): 11–28.

8. To my essay on *The Clouds*, I added a sentence about the September 11 strikes, since the torching of Socrates's School now seemed tragic, not comic.

are now called his works are the works of a Socrates made young and beautiful. Farewell and believe. (*Epistle* II)

Philosophers, Plato concedes, do risk spiritual parricide (*Sophist*, 241*d*) but Plato's own desire was to retrieve, not destroy, his spiritual father Socrates and to channel his still evolving voice. In Plato's deed, we find the beginning of the humanities and the archetype, perhaps, of all hermeneutic retrieval. We hope that the best of our past will emerge young and beautiful again.

ACKNOWLEDGMENTS

I would like to thank Arthur Dolsen, whose recitations in Greek are so memorable, for discussing the translations in this manuscript; Sharon Sieber, for suggestions regarding synchronicities and help with word-processing; and Tracy Montgomery for many pertinent and valuable comments and suggestions. A sabbatical leave from Idaho State University provided an opportunity to begin this manuscript. The help and inspiration of Judith Hutton has been indispensable.

www.ingramcontent.com/pod-product-compliance
Lightning Source LLC
Chambersburg PA
CBHW030114170426
43198CB00009B/624